ARRIVAL PRESS

THE ARRIVAL PRESS

SPRING POETRY COLLECTION

Edited

By

TIM SHARP

First published in Great Britain in 1996 by
ARRIVAL PRESS
1 - 2 Wainman Road, Woodston,
Peterborough, PE2 7BU

HB ISBN 1 85786 374 7
SB ISBN 1 85786 369 0

Foreword

The Arrival Press Spring Collection contains a wide variety of verse by people from all walks of life, spanning a wide age group.

Whilst editing this book I found the topics gave a broad outlook on life in general from happiness to sadness, beauty and war.

All in all a very entertaining anthology worth reading over and over again.

Tim Sharp
Editor

CONTENTS

TEARS

Tears of sadness and tears of joy
Tears that are falling for my little boy
My eyes are o'erflowing but what can I do
To make you aware of my love for you?

Your hands are so tiny your eyes are so blue
Your hair is like silk your skin is brand new
What have I done in bringing you here
To a world without love and one filled with fear?

How can I shelter one so tender and dear
From the hate of mankind in another new year?
Where there's no shelter for our children tho' oh so young
And who will then care when the last song is sung?

You arrived like an angel to a world full of sin
And I opened my heart and let you come in
With your heart and your soul so full of trust
I gave you a world full of hate and of lust

All that I have is a few very short years
To save you from harm and all of the tears
Then you'll be a man and live your own life
To start over again with your very own wife

Until then my dear son I will be by your side
I won't tell you lies or e'en try to hide
The truth from your eyes nor from your ears
Tho' it will be painful over the years

And yes once again my eyes fill with tears
When I hear the sweet sound of your voice in my ears
So don't be afraid my beautiful son
To cry for a world of which you are one

Fiona Higgins

RESTLESS SPIRIT

Oh restless spirit keep
My feet on the ground
Don't let me go wandering
Where I can't be found,
My restless mind tell
My feet to go
Somewhere out there
Where I don't know,
I'd like to fly
With wings on my heels
To faraway places
Whenever I feel,
The urge to go wandering
Away from the crowds
Take over my thoughts
And knows no bounds,
So my wandering spirit
When you've had enough
Make sure I come home
To the one that I love.

P G Locke

FALLING OUT OF LOVE

I can only feel love
If my heart is truly in it
I can only feel love
For the time that I am in it

And like the fall
Into summer
When the rain comes down
It's all eventually over
So when the blow comes to blow
All good things may go

And outside the world
May come without seeing
But there's changes
Every day for as
Long as we are living

Debra Webb

STRESS-FREE

If you rise early go out and meet the new day
Pleasure it brings treasures you find
A sprinkling of stars in a blue velvet sky
Cobwebs hang like gossamer lace of every kind

Dew shining on the grass rivals any jewel in the crown
Birch trees standing so straight clothed in pure silver and gold
The scent of wild roses on hedgerows profuse
A lark so high its song so bold.

Willows dipping in a fast-running stream
Sounding like distant clock chimes
Silhouetted hills come into view
Moss covered stones with no distinct lines

Pathways black with sudden rain
Ducklings that splash around reeds so tall
A dragonfly waits for the sun to return
A flash of blue as a kingfisher hears her mate call.

Every season has its magic
The next one as much as the one that has been
A rainbow brightens the now blue sky
Brilliant colours that blend with every scene.

Hilda Waugh

ODE TO A DARLING GRAND-DAUGHTER

With your face so fair and your eyes of deep blue
You look like a cherub, you act like one too
When at night, in your cot, in deep slumber you lay,
Tired from your playing and learning all day.
Your grin is infectious, that angelic smile
Could charm all the devils in hell for a while.
Your days are all filled with experiences new,
You're learning more words, you now know quite a few.
You have not learned to walk yet, just crawl on the floor,
Then pull out some toys, then some more and some more.
When I call round to see you I get a big kiss,
Or a bang on the face as your frequently miss.
You wave me hello and you wave me goodbye,
And sometimes, when I've got to go home you cry.
You are just one of millions who're born every year,
But to me you're the 'one in a million' my dear.

Brenda Spencer

THE GIRL IN THE GRAVEYARD

When winds blow cold, she is icy alone;
Frost-bitten chrysanthemums at her feet.
The pallid chill would suggest she is stone,
Emaciated by the lack of heat.
But yet when she smiles her warmth is passed on
To the enticed clandestine observer.
Deathly black hair and the eyes of a song
Attract life in a passionate fever.
Oh why can't she see, insentient queen -
Her glowing frigidity sorrows me -
That such pulchritude pulls and tends to wean
Away the spirit of people once free:
To a level of love too sharp to bear;
I pray release us, ice maiden so fair.

Gareth Allen

4

UNTITLED

Where is the fun in being a mum
If what I hear is true.
It's 'oh shut up' 'get out' 'I won't'
Or simply 'I hate you.'
We spend our days in childish play
When they are very young
Then as they grow, it's 'you don't know'
And efforts go unsung.
We've gone without, there is no doubt,
In our parental quest
But gratitude's no attitude
For teens who think they're best.
So, mother's job is over.
Don't try to help or guide,
Just wonder why you bother,
When no-one's on your side.

Maureen Butcher

RECOVERY

Eyes half closed, flabby jowl silent, tongue the only life sign.
Foul breath, entwined with stale saliva, gelling on cold lino.
Strong gait halted in the main, only a flicker
of nerves now and again.
Shimmering kaleidoscope of black and tan.
Sweat patches surfacing where they can.
The cut is clean and true worked by
skilled hand on you.
Come dawn pain will inflict its vicious self.
For now rest - in drug induced peace.
Ignorant of the motherhood taken from you.

Sue Neale

GIVE ME BACK MY COUNTRY

Give me back my country as it used to be
When many roads were traffic-free
And the air was pure and clean.
Give me back the freedom to roam the country lanes
The open field of grasses green
Where picnic parties could be seen and
Children could safely play and gather flowers as they may
Cowslips, buttercups, harebells too
Along with tall white pennymoons.
Give me back our lovely woods
Where bluebells, in abundance grew
Like a velvet carpet softly spread with morning dew.

Bring me back my country with its slow and steady pace
Before it raced along at speed
Towards its never ending greed.
Give me back the home life when families were as one
And folks had time to chat and care
And courtesy was everywhere
If only the powers that be could retract the damage they have done
To try again with great endeavour
And give me back my country before it's gone forever.

Mona Skirving

THE PHOENIX

The phoenix rises
from the flames,
memory dulls
of the pain
newness awakes
with the awakening.

Naked I stand
new life warming
once darkened eyes
a smile of victory
as shadows flee
no more lies
no longer fear
as the phoenix stand I here.

Derrin Gaskell

CRUFTS

I wish I were a mongrel
Without a pedigree,
I wish that I were ugly,
As scruffy as can be.

Then I could go rabbiting,
Rolling in the mud,
Messing up my silky coat,
I'd feel so very good.

Oh, how I hate that grooming kit
That's supposed to make me smart,
As for that first prize rosette,
It makes me look a tart.

Then there's all that dieting,
That delicate cuisine;
One tasty juicy butcher's bone
Makes that lot seem obscene.

Here comes that poncy judging man,
I'd love to bite his arm,
Instead, I 'spect I shall exert
All my doggie charm!

Jean Adams

THE BIONIC MAN
(Dedicated to the Chairman of the Clay Pigeon Shoot)

Our Chairman is a man of great renown
The likes of him could not be found
He's a man with ever winning smile
The very devil he could beguile
He has great measure of success
And never leaves things in a mess
Everything he goes to do
Is nearly equalled by a few
He's a true-born sportsman all the way
And likes to shoot the birds of clay
To see them spinning through the air
Is a sight for him beyond compare
And when he's asked to take the stand
His shooting style is mighty grand
He calls the birds there on his sight
Bang, bang. They're powered out of flight
Now he's some shooter make no mistake
Compared with him great shots are fake
He could be our next Olympic seed
But he very humbly pays no heed
Friends and guests one and all
He's our host tonight at the shootball
He has organised this great event
To please us all on pleasure bent
He couldn't be the man he is
Without a wife that is all his
She's a lady fair and serene
And inspires him to reign supreme.
With thankfulness we'll drink a toast,
To our delightful charming host.

Jack Howie

THE FINAL CURTAIN, DEATH CALLS

When will it come?
Will we know?
Or will it suddenly strike?
The news has been given
My time is nearly up.
How can I face it?
What will help?

Now is the time to say goodbyes
Straighten up my affairs
Say my fond farewells to one and all.

I am frightened.
What will it feel like?
Will it hurt, will I know?
Death is awesome or is it!
Once at peace with all,
I can accept that the final curtain has come.
What will it be like on the other side?
Will I meet family and friends?

I am ready, the time has come.
My number's up.
Everyone has been so kind
Good bye, farewell. I'm off to fresher fields.
Pain has gone. Release is here.

Bridget Taylor

SUZY

Oh good and faithful, loving friend
My heart is heavy, your life now at an end.

Suzy, so kind, soft and gentle, full of life and go.
To play your favourite game of retrieve and throw
Humans were made, just for sticks and balls to hurl.
Your marking's so different, black eye, white coated girl.

We had so much fun, you and me, playing, going for a walk.
To find a scent, rabbit, squirrel, your nose would stalk.
Then you were off, running and chasing your hoped for prey,
But you always returned to your mistress, to love and obey.

Intelligent and knowing, alert, wise canine beast,
Training, so easy, you were a champion at least.
Wagging tail, smiling face. Once abandoned, full of fears.
Happy, now rescued for the rest of your seven years.

Oh faithful friend, your loving eyes, endearing ways,
Nudging my arm to stroke and pat you, many happy days.
Watching, waiting by the window, looking for me to come home.
Guarding, trusting, loving me, with you I was never alone.

Never complaining, ever accepting, faithful hound.
Whatever my mood, your devotion always sure and sound.
Loyal, true, trusty dog, playmate, chum, never failing friend.
My loving companion, why must your life come to its end?

The house so still, empty of your movements and sound
I open the door, expecting to spy you on the ground.
But no, I am disappointed, seeing only the empty space,
Uninhabited, bare, where once I looked upon your face.

My heart is hurting, as my grateful thanks I send,
To Suzy, my dog, a good and faithful, loving friend.

Esmé E Wilson

THE GROWTH OF THE MOTOR CAR

The car is such a useful thing,
So much pleasure does it bring.
Some families have three or four,
And rarely walk far from their door.

It's more than a century when cars first appeared
And the countryside has fast disappeared
Miles of motorway and trunk roads we've had to build
And as fast as we've done so, they're rapidly filled.

The open road too is fast disappearing
So many cars keep rapidly appearing
I wonder if there is a simple solution
To all this congestion and poisonous pollution?

It's not as though motoring is nowadays cheap
From motorists there is hardly a peep
But must have their cars whatever the price
They'll buy a brand new one without thinking twice.

In cities the streets are blocked up each day
You can only move slowly and certainly can't stay
Car parks are full and in the street, if you stop
You'll soon be spotted by a warden or cop.

Cars are being banned from the city centre
Such streets will be only for shoppers to venture
That makes for more pleasantness in the town
And helps to keep many accidents down.

We shall have to accept more severe restriction
To run our cars without undue friction
Possibly petrol and diesel may have to be banned
And electricity or some other fuel planned.

W M Jones

VERTIGO

I've left it too late -
Left the deciding match to Fate -
And lost, ten - nil . . .
I scrabble frantically in the cupboard,
Boxes and bottles falling about my head.
The world flickers around
Like a bad film reel.
Somewhere in this damn cupboard
A small box holds my salvation.
I crawl around now, trying to ensure
That it's not among the medicinal debris
Lying on the floor. No luck.
Hurling the litter back into the cupboard
With the world flying in circles
My hand touches,
Clutches,
A small box -
For God's sake, what's it doing
So far back?
My fingers fumble to eject
The tiny tablets from their shiny foil.
Urgently, I shove them under my top lip
And swiftly stumble
To the friendly settee
Where the ground falls away from beneath my feet,
But at least the world
Will stay still for me.

Ann Markey

REACHING OUT

Heard You cured the sick.
Made the blind to see.
Healed the lame.
What can You do for me,
for this soul of mine . . . ?

I hear You give the
bread of life for free,
would You give it to me . . . ?

I shed a tear for the pain
I've caused.
For the hurt I didn't care about.
Can You ease this pain . . . ?

Could You bless me for all my sins?
And be forgiving?
Could You smile on me,
as I fall on my knees
to kneel at Your feet.

Where do I go from here -
could You show me the way?
Can You help me to live
my life the way I should,
from day to day . . . ?

What can I do to learn from my
ways?
Could You teach me?
Help me to find what's missing
what isn't there.
To show people that I care . . .
can I let You take it from there . . . ?

Christine Jackson

DEADLY DEALING

The face is staring, the eyes are fixed
They all look on, emotions mixed
Eyes closed, yesteryear, and there you are
A catalyst of pleasure, joy beyond measure
Sweet little face, full of trust
A new day dawning, the peace of dusk
A love that comes from deep within
Spilling to pastures, nurturing
The yellow yarrow, the cream of the clover
Now seventeen, it's almost over
Touched by the pedlar, outwith reason's reach
The apple blemished, the owl's shriek
The hapless mouse goes scurrying by
The talons are poised, his fate is nigh
Panicked and anxious and fraught with despair
The feelings numbed, see the eyes stare
Nibbled and gnawed and spat out to claim
A vacant space in life's murkiest drain
Begins the turbulent downward spin
The innocents pulled along within
Sighs, sobs and senses reeling
Against this monstrous evil dealing
The bark is peeling, see the boughs droop,
The shoulders of parents visibly stoop.

Jacqueline D Rhodes

HAPPY HOLOGRAM

It begins
with pins
on my skin.

And then it cuts
my bones jut
deep gashes over my whole body.

I'm exposed, but
I laugh composed
as the blood pours. Unnoticed.

Naked in the rain
I wish away this blatant pain.

I smile.
Happy hologram.

Claire Grace

HOMELAND?

The fall of the daughter, the child that you slaughter,
In crimson and scarlet the blood on the mortar.
The cheat and the stealing of all social feeling;
Enforcing destruction through white powder dealing.
The loss of the tree, pollution of sea, the rampant injustice
Of laws you decree.
The cry for equality - hypocritical jollity,
Dreamed in the bar of the house of frivolity.
The wig of induction, the gavel of seduction,
That hammers the bribes into lives of corruption.
The key of warder, the cell of the boarder,
Have poverty and crime reached the same basic order?
The stench of the bigot, the curse of the faggot,
Who pimps and corrupts like some deep delving maggot.
The wealth of the traitor, the crime instigator,
Who fingers the pauper - protection for favour.
The bone of contention, the air of redemption,
That graces the face when a death is to mention.
The lines of the crone, the chair or the throne?
The greed and depravity of England my home.

C Gardiner

BEST FRIENDS

Best friends are like paper and glue,
That's what we are - me and you,
You're always there for me, when I'm blue,
'Cos we're best friends - me and you.

The minute I met you I knew you were the one,
Who'd cheer me up, when I'm glum,
We'll stay together and face life yet to come,
'Cos we're best friends and we'll have some fun.

You've given me confidence, light and hope,
You've shown me what friends are, and really cool jokes,
You've told me secrets, so I can now cope,
'Cos we're best friends like lemonade and coke.

You and me are like paper and glue,
Paper and glue are like me and you.

Emily Buckman-Drage

LBSL (HYPOGLYCAEMIA)
(Written on the bog at ASDA)

Sweating, screaming, breathing, dreaming.
Give me food and I'll stop bleeding.
Spaced out, pale and unaware,
Do I need help or just someone to care?
Inhale the sadness that covers our souls,
Exhale the madness that no one knows.
I'm no longer trying,
But inside I'm crying
And slowly,
I can feel myself dying.

Gary Symington

VICTORIAN LOVE

(In memory of William, aged 3 years)

Within high turret walls, the house, a memento once kept!
From a bygone age, a trinket, of one who wept,
For William, death came at only three years,
His Mother's love, conveyed in pearls for tears.

Lustrous and tiny, set around a brooch of mock gold,
Seed pearls stand for tears, so I've been told.
In their midst lies a curl, the colour of ripe corn,
A tress, off the babe she did mourn.

For ended her world, one summer of yesteryear,
When birdsong filled an air so clear.
Who can guess at her despair?
Forsaken, by the child with golden hair.

In remembrance then of the son she bore,
This memorial brooch she always wore.
Of pensive thoughts, and tears, for the child who died,
'Time would heal,' said they, 'a gap so wide.'

Nigh over a hundred years flew by,
Forgotten was she, and William no more than a sigh,
Their world had gone forever more,
Left, wrapped in a trinket, which once at heartstrings tore.

For sale, came the house within high walls of stone,
All items went, from her turreted home.
Seasons turned, again the brooch was sold,
Their love locked in, now my trinket of mock gold.

Jennifer Neville

LAMENTABLE STATE OF AFFAIRS

My bank manager has the most annoying habit
For whenever I see him he begins to rabbit
and waffle about
the state of my account
and how, to him,
the figures look grim
and how I seldom
put in,
more than I take out.
But with well practised deceptive ease,
I smile and say . . . puh . . . lease!
There is no need of such concern
For, as you will no doubt learn,
A sizeable payment to me is now due
and as soon as I get it
I'll hand it to you,
Meantime there's a new venture
I really must pursue
So, be a good chap
and extend my credit,
(For we must give credit
where credit is due)
I don't ask for the earth
But for what it is worth
It would be most helpful
to have the wherewithal,
So . . . perhaps you'll advance me
a mere hundred or two?

A B LeGrey

18

SIX DAYS THAT CHANGED MY LIFE

Days full of joy and hundred interests sharing
Our minds enmeshed and bodies intertwined.
I, with my pain, not finding walking easy.
You with bereavement gnawing still your mind.
And yet there was joy, and ev'n a kind of healing
Such as may come to suff'ring human-kind.
You so concerned, solicitous and caring.
I with emotions I never thought to find.

Doreen Allison

MEDIA MAN

There seems a need for crystal clarity,
On issues concerning sexuality.
Advising couples on love-making positions
Letting go anxieties, releasing inhibitions.

A man in 1996
Would find it extremely hard to miss,
The strategic place that causes bliss,
That all-important clitoris.

The media suggests a man is pathetic,
If he can't stay the distance - be sexually athletic.

But relax all you lads, do not despair,
This idea is false, it's really unfair,
A real man is someone who looks after his own,
Provides them food and a comfortable home.
So love your family and love your wife,
And you'll be able to love your life.

Paul Perry

TRAGEDY

I sit in the chapel,
My mate by my side.
I'm sitting and sweating,
I wait for my bride.
The flowers at the altar
Are virgin and sweet.
I'm sitting and thinking,
'The world's at my feet!'

And soon she will enter,
And walk down the aisle.
A vision of beauty,
A sight to beguile!
And soon will the organ
Play 'O Promise Me',
And we'll stand together,
Forever to be!

Then out on the sidewalk
The sound of a shot!
But no-one takes notice
It happens a lot!
Some drunken young 'puncher'
Is having his fun,
He's jus' celebratin'
And flashin' his gun!

A woman is screaming
Out there, in the sun,
And men are a'cursing,
So outside I run!
My skin is a'crawling,
For there in the street,
My bride, in her trousseau,
Lies dead at my feet!

I sit in the chapel,
My mate by my side.
Up there is a coffin,
And in it, my bride!
The bell in the tower,
Has started to toll,
I'll look for that 'cowboy',
Then *God help his soul!*

Stanley Gott

UNTITLED

My imagination is running high,
I am in the clouds sailing,
On my thoughts, my wishes,
My life is changing,
I am being given a gift
To know, and share and love.

There is realisation
Of what matters in this world
Of what is crucial in my life.
I want to open my soul
To encompass it all, the happy and the sad,
I am exhilarated by my freedom
Like a child running through the waves on an empty beach,
I am washed and clean, my understanding clear.

My strength is my stability,
Making me walk carefully with my new-found self
Like a full glass being gingerly carried along
I do not wish to spill these precious feelings.
I can look at the sky and know that is all I need
To inspire me to live another day, to take on this life,
A life that has been given to me a second time
I treasure it and trust my intuition to guide me well.

Lindsey O'Hara

WHEN I'M GONE

When time betrays my beating heart,
And angels wave me home,
I'll lose the memory of each part,
Of the love we called our own,
No more the vision of your face,
And the smile that from it shone,
When Heaven is my resting place,
Earthly beauty will be gone.

Remember me with all your love,
Or forget me if you will,
A mansion waits for me above,
There's no cause for tears to spill,
No reason for my feeling scared,
When I rise beyond the blue,
For eternal love I am prepared,
By the time I spent with you.

Never wish that I was there,
To see each coming morn,
In a world which suffers doubt and fear,
Where goodness suffers scorn,
'Tis nothing but a testing ground,
I hope you'll come to see,
The happy truth that I have found,
Then you can follow me.

A Pay

THE SEA AND ME

I'm like the sea,
Strong and wild,
I love the sea,
It's like me.

I'm like the sea,
Mysterious and strange,
I love the sea,
It's just like me.

I'm like the sea,
Wild and dangerous,
I love the sea,
It's exactly like me.

Melinda Harris

THIS LOVE, REJOICE

I love your eyes
They thrill me so
Your deep red lips
Your cheeks that glow
The way you move
The way you walk
I almost cartwheel when you talk

Your soft-tone words
And angel voice
My heart expands
And holds its poise
My tongue gets tied
I'm filled with joy
These words are true
This love, Rejoice

Tony Reid

BUSY BUSY

They're rushing here and there're rushing there
Rushing mostly everywhere
Never a minute morn or night
Then into bed and then sleep tight.

Morning comes in the same big rush
Always at it one big push
Never time to think of self
So put your worries on the shelf

Every thing comes to those who wait
Be it early or be it late.

Barbara Dearness

DREAM COTTAGE

A cottage is a charming place,
Showing the world such a cosy face.
With walls that are built of thick, stout stones
Or colourwashed in pastel tones.
With sparkling windows that quaintly peep
From under the eaves of a roof thatched deep.
Around the doorway rambling roses grow
And the garden is like a flower show
With old-fashioned flowers growing in profusion
All scents and colours in gay confusion.
Imagine yourself spending happy hours there,
Just pottering about with time to spare.
Inside, latched wooden doors into snug rooms go,
With ingle nooks and oak beams and ceilings low.
Imagine yourself on a cold winter's night,
Chair drawn up to the hearth where logs burn bright.
Outside life is lived mainly in the fast lane
But inside a cottage peace and tranquillity reign.

J Jackson

NOBODY LOVES ME

I'm alone, lost in a barbaric waste ground,
I wander deserted streets looking for a home,
Loneliness is nothing new to me, as I have found,
I cower in a corner taking shelter from the rain,
I scavenge through humans' rubbish with nothing to gain,
Sometimes there is kindness, a bone, a treat,
Other times I'm frightened when the dog catcher's on the street,
At night I curl up in a doorway warmed by the heat,
In the morning I'm damp from my head to my feet,
I see children with their pets happy and free,
I'm bruised and beaten 'cause nobody loves me.

Melisa A Owen

YOUR LOVE

With your love wrapped around me
Like a well-worn coat
Your presence does surround me
Like a scarf around my throat
My eyes seek out yours
From several thousand other
Our love is not dissimilar
To a son's love for his mother
I don't need to tell you
That you are my universe
I just need to show you
You could do a lot worse
So settle down around me
Let's begin a brand new life
You can be my husband
And I will be your wife.

Rachel Taylor

LIZARD

Lizard in the hot sun
 On a hot rock
  Sunbathing daily
   But not getting brown
    Darting quick-quickly
     Away from human hand
      Little comic reptile
       Of ages gone by

Lizard at the corner
 Of my eye
  Seen-not-seen
   Like a camera shutter
    Like a flash of lightning
     On a hot night
      Sign of summer
       And gaudy hats

Lizard silent there
 Sunning your lazy body
  I wrote you a poem
   Because no-one else did
    And lizard contented
     In the drenching heat
      I want to be a lizard
       Next time round

Bridget Rayner

FANTASIES OF A CHILD

The bed where I sleep is a spaceship or raft
My brother a monster who sometimes acts daft
The cat is a creature that talks in the night
She lays by my bedside in the moonlight
Our garden a jungle that I must explore
The school is a workplace a playhouse and more
The days are all one the season's the same
I feel hot then cold and it's Christmas again
The clock in the hallway it ticks then it chimes
It tells me I'm tired and it's nearly bedtime
The coal in the fireplace glows at my feet
A world of wonder from which I feel heat
The shapes and the figures that my eyes can see
Of animals and ships and of giant oak trees
The puffs of white cloud that move over my head form
                            mountains and shapes in the sky
And beyond all the shapes and above the blue light rests
                            the heavens above us on high
As I lay within my warm sheets my fantasies run wild
I want to get big I want to grow up but still always
                            remain just a child

Howard Oates

PASSING

The pain and the strain is sometimes too much,
I've seen it all before and I'll see it again,
But I need my cares caressing with your velvet touch,
You're all I want and all I need to ease my pain,

Through whispering whistling winds I hear your call,
I know the release of death is relief to your aching heart,
So the sweet sleeping sickness continues my fall,
Swaying side to side, I view my sad life before I depart.

Karen Greatbatch

27

BEING A MUM

Being a mum is a blessing from God
Giving pleasure compared with no other
From that moment your baby is thrust in your arms
You begin to face life as a mother

That darling sweet angel we see in his cot
Admired so by family and friends
That beautiful boy, his mum's pride and joy
Will play havoc before the day ends

He's toddling now, oh, what a big boy
Your trouble's about to begin
For nothing is safe in the home any more
From the moment that rascal comes in

How gorgeous he looks in his new suit of clothes
His mum shows him off with great pleasure
The suit cost a fortune she could ill afford
But nothing's too good for her treasure

An hour or so later, her small son appears
His new suit all covered in grease
He's been helping Daddy, lay under the car
To give Mummy just an hour's peace

The great day approaches when he begins school
At last Mum can have some more leisure
But she watches the clock and longs for the time
That will give her the ultimate pleasure

The day was so lonesome when he was away
With no-one to cuddle or chide
That day she had promised to do her own thing
Was lost without him by her side

Yes, being a mum is a blessing indeed
And in spite of the troubles and strife
Just being a mum, I think you'll agree
Are the happiest days of your life.

G A Bonsen

UNTITLED

Watching now the summer fly
and the sun rise lower in the sky
the crystal light, with brittle fingers
upon each branch and twig lingers,
and tries to break the frost which clings
like armour to the trees' brown skins.
The last remaining golden leaves
like a lover to their partner cleaves,
and trembling on the boughs, though frail
resist the unrelenting gale,
which whips his hurried way across
the trees, and lake and grass and moss,
and breaks upon my great glass windows
howling, writhing in gusty death throes.
Till stopped upon this malevolent course
it drops, now spent of all its force.
Then as a patient, who after a fever sleeps
the breeze, gently about the stiff trunks sweeps
gathering the leaves twitching upon the floor
which in anger, from their perches tore.
Across the clear expansive sky
the migrating birds in formation fly,
like an arrow-head they quickly pass
in search of lands where summer lasts.
And so daily before my view
Nature's pageant starts anew.

B Williams

NIGHT-WALKING

Lonely, sad old nights
when you feel like you've no home,
You walk the empty streets
taking your blues for a stroll.

Bright rooms entice your eyes:
people sharing a TV screen;
autumn trees wave slowly across the streetlights
You've no shadow and no substance here.

A few hours before, you were moving in each other's time;
entwined, locked, breathless, escaping the world,
time racing;
no time at all;
and now you're alone, left with the notes, but no tune,
and you can hardly remember how it goes -
you can't play it on your own.

So you stalk the sad old streets
searching for some music;
dragging your blues through the rain,
empty and helpless as Hell only knows.

Meena Cochon

GHOSTS

One night when I was going to bed
I got an awful fright
For when I turned and had a look,
I seen a ghastly sight.

There was a vampire and a ghost
A wolfman, a Frankenstein.
They all looked very scary,
All standing in a line.

They started dancing all around,
And jumping on the bed,
It was as if they were alive,
But they all were - *dead!*

Suddenly, they all disappeared
They vanished like cats' cream,
Then I just opened up my eyes,
And found it was a dream.

Kristopher Jack

JUNIOR SCHOOL DAYS

At the age of five I started school,
My brother was already there,
He's a little bit older than me you see
And I suppose I was in his care.
I don't remember my first day
So I couldn't have been worried at all,
And everything must have been alright
But I simply don't recall.
It was a nice little school in the Lower Wyche
For children from five to fourteen.
It had three lady teachers, I remember them still
Miss Plumb, Miss Creese and Miss Joan Till,
And a kindly headmaster who wielded the cane,
He was a friend of my father and called Mr Staines.
I made new friends, some I still see today,
I'd visit their homes and together we'd play,
There was Marjorie and Barbara and Beth as well
We had lots of fun until teacher rang the bell,
Then back into class we all had to run,
Yes, I remember Junior School as a whole load of fun.

Valerie Lowe

SEASONS

The seasons change as nature unfolds,
The colourful mystery of power untold,
Unknown timing for magnificent change,
Unknown the power, how to explain.

The sweeping strokes of the master's brush,
Great scenes change with a single touch,
From brilliant colours to browns and greys,
Forever changing, never stays.

The sun's bright rays and tanning tone,
Spread far and wide for nature's poem,
Another stroke, another scene,
The splash of colour where he's been.

Leaves that tumble from the trees,
To come again with soft spring breeze,
The white of snow that melts away,
The rains that come and floods that stay.

Summer, autumn, winter, spring,
The tender strokes they sometimes bring,
Sometimes the strokes become so strong,
That seasons tarry far too long.

As seasons pass and go we see,
The artist's work with licence free,
With these great scenes he leaves behind,
His changing tapestries for all mankind.

B K Williams

UNTITLED

We once were together but now you are gone,
Although I still worship the ground you walk on,
You hate me, I love you, it's a one-sided thing,
Forever I'll love you so I'll keep trying,
I've asked you out, you said I don't know,
Eventually your answer will be no.
You've done it before I guess I just do not learn,
To be held in your arms again I yearn.
If a miracle could happen and my dreams come true,
All I'd want is to be loved by you.
I can't get you out of my head,
I dream of you when I'm in bed,
I'm crazy about you,
Do you feel that way too?
I dream of us together,
We'd fall out never,
You hold my hand and flirt you see,
Don't you realise what that does to me?
If you showed your feeling maybe we'd be together once more,
And mend my heart which you once tore,
That would never happen 'cos you hate me so much,
To kiss you and hold you or even to touch,
Forget him, people say, easier said than done,
If you love me again we could have lots of fun.

Laura Kingswood (14)

BANGOR

Belfast people came to town
because it was within their reach
They don't come any more
we took away the beach.

You could see them on a summer's day
with bucket and spade in hand
Then the tears filled their eyes
they could not see the sand.

The putting green around the clock
was really good fun for all
Now they see to their surprise
a car park behind the wall.

A building sprang up in plain view
not a pretty sight to see
They didn't need permission
not like you me.

The moral of my poem is
and it's not really funny
They took away the sea and and
and did it with our *money.*

Maurice Robinson

BUTTERFLY DREAMS

Butterfly - spread your wings
      and fly away:
I long to be a butterfly
      painted black!
Caught in the wind you toss,
Powder falls to the floor.
Oh butterfly - poor butterfly!

Butterfly take my dreams
          and fly away:
Like you I fly -
          in my dreams.
Pretty butterfly;
Gentle butterfly!
Fly - fly and soar,
Each flower is my dream.
          Oh butterfly:
          Poor butterfly.

Jessica Bonney (17)

DESTROYING THE OZONE

The planet earth will burn itself out
Of that fact there can be no doubt
But must we help it on its way
By destroying the ozone every day?

We're killing ourselves with out own pollution
We must stop it now and find a solution
The hole we've created in the sky
We must mend or surely die

By destroying the ozone every day
The death of our planet's the price we'll pay
We must join together to show we all care
Or there will be no future for us to share

The powers that be must be made to believe
Before there's no more air to breathe
Before the ozone gets too thin
This fight for our planet we must win

Some say the end of the world is nigh
Just stop for a moment and ask yourself *why?*

Robert Steen McDougall

UNDERNEATH THESE SCOTTISH SKIES

Underneath these Scottish skies
A feast for any Scotsman's eyes
The sun reflects upon the ledge
Of the weary, lapping water's edge
The greatest sight you've ever seen
The hills and vales alive in green
Whispering winds, a chill in the air
Resounding through trees, here and there.

Underneath, as the Lord watches over
The children laugh, dancing in the clover
Their games of bravery give warming to them
A feeling to echo all great hearts of men
One day, this land will be free
For Scotland is more than all that we see . . .
It's a feeling, inside, that makes us proud
It can make a whisper, ring true and loud.

Underneath the stars above
All of our kinsmen are bonded with love
A love for all, and one, it seems
Is all that will liberate our dreams
As skies above, grow tired and cold
When I am dying, crying and old
I'll gaze beneath these Scottish skies
A feast for any Scotsman's eyes.

C Poynter

CECIL PERCHOUSE

His best friend was a louse.
He didn't live in a house.
He yearned for a pair of shoes,
So he gambled his stolen fiver -
Praying he wouldn't lose.
Of course though he did, poor kid.
He dragged his tired feet back down to Black Street
And searched for a dry cardboard box.
As he prayed desperately for sleep
He couldn't help but to weep
At the trouble he'd got into so deep.
One year so rich, the next in a ditch.
So he decided to climb out again.
He stole some money from an easy target shop
And set up a market stall.
It wasn't really much
But it got him back in touch
With the real world once and for all.
Every day was a high, as he sat thinking he'd sigh
At the simple joy he had made for himself.
Yet the light turned to black
As he suffered a heart attack
Because of the excitement in his heart every day.
At least it was happiness that sent Cecil on his way.

Marianne Redfern

MARS

Way beyond the Jupiter stars
Lies the distant planet Mars.
Hanging in space turning around,
Blood red colour never a sound.

Spin in orbit, rockets down,
Eerie surface, craggy mounds.
Mountains soar in ruddy hue,
Longest day and shortest blue.

The fissure opened crevasse snaked,
Crossing barren river baked.
Buggy bounce in forward gear,
Sunlight glare in atmosphere.

Very still with dusty boots,
Hiss of air in pressure suits.
System crackle radio call,
Tender steps and shadow tall.

Footprint pattern on desert beach,
Far below the valley reach.
Sweating now inside the mask,
Camera on a labour's task.

Mission over flag on hill.
Final countdown blast-off pill.
Test the switches feel the pull,
Strapped in tight ignition full.

Engine shut down, frantic base,
Hatches open smile on face.
Circuits dead and air is past,
Planet Mars I'm home at last.

Nick Woods

LOST CAUSE

I had thought a lot about love and life
And pondered the question which girl to wife.

The mumsy blonde with confidence lacking
The Essex girl with immaculate packing.

The office spy with long nails short hair
The Amazon girl tall and fair.

The revenue girl wild and free
Only one wife why not three?

Though as I sat and stared around,
My feet once again touched reality ground.

Down from the clouds the dreams and lust,
Back to this earthly core's toil and dust.

So back to work my mind I turned
All thoughts of women from my head I spurned.

The hours flew by and my bachelor pad called
But into my thoughts another angel stalled.

Brunette and gentile a lady to her centre
I felt in my mind a question enter.

So taking courage and purpose of will
I asked her name, a smile I'm Gill.

We spoke and laughed, teased and mused
But then another question lit my fuse.

So what are you doing, are you free?
I'm married, two kids and off home to tea.

John Stewart Cameron

BRITISH FOOD

While walking round a superstore
It made me think of days of yore
Although fast food some say is good
What's happened to our Yorkshire pud?
It's in the freezer there to see
In frozen packs good gracious me
My mum would say what a disgrace
The rubbish bin's the proper place
There's pastry mix and scone mix and sauces by the score
Tinned meat and ready dinners need I tell you more?
If food's not got a fancy name it's doomed before the start
But tell me what on earth is wrong with good old treacle tart?
We had tripe, black pudding trotters and even gooseberry fool
Mum's steak and kidney pudding really made one drool
Then I got to thinking when I was first a bride
I had rows of jams and pickles standing side by side
When I stood and looked at them ready on the shelf
The pride I had in telling friends I made them all myself
So get into the kitchen when next you have a guest
Let the mixer do some work it's had many years of rest
You'd save a bit of money and it would do you good
I'm sure you would agree with me
There's nowt like British food.

Barbara Payne

TOGETHER

I want to die happy, and not when I'm sad
I want you to love me and be by my side,
I want you to hear me when eveyone's deaf
And to stay at my side when I've nobody left.

Rachael Armitage

40

A NAME AND NUMBER

I lie here in a heavy slumber,
I think I'm just a name and number,
And then I hear a familiar voice,
And think do I really have a choice?

'Ooh! He's cute and wide awake,'
I'm given a tickle and a shake,
Why do they make a fuss of me?
Particularly when granny comes for tea?

She knows nothing about my life,
My aching gums cause trouble and strife,
Nappy changing, no choice of food,
I have to take the bad and good.

But they tell me it won't always be,
Like this when granny comes for tea,
When I grow up she'll take me out,
And then she'll let me run about.

I'll climb on rocks and jump off swings,
I'll play with toys and lots of things,
That older children often do,
I'll even go off to the zoo.

So when will this excitement start?
I want to join in and take part
In all this fun and noisy games,
Make new friends and learn their names.

'In all good time, my dear child,
You'll run about and go quite wild,
Until then just enjoy your slumber,
For you're not just a name and number.'

Catherine E Craft

NOT TO MENTION THE PRIMROSES AND VIOLETS

Steep-stumbling white water,
The pearly, the pure, so clear in its course;
Silver glints, deep dimples,
Marbled moss, in love, cocooning crag -
Mere man dwarfing, wayfaring.
New fern-fronds come curled,
Atop brown-bearded, strong stems,
Gold and brown, gold and brown.

Tree-crooks, and rock-tops, polypoded;
Breath-taking the leaves, miracle-lifted
Foetus-fresh, unchanged from heaven's own mint.

The understorey
Blue-dappled by hyacinth's bells,
All stitched with white -
Virgin-white, from stitchwort's cheery
Two-pronged-petal's salute,
Fickle fingers daintily dipped
As they sip the spring air.

Blackbird the lyre; Jenny-
Wren chorus, the groupies, backing,
Paradise whistle-stop, pop-top,
Laudate Dominum

W A Saxton

UNTITLED

The strife and panic in our world today
The sound of guns though far away
The loudening beat of the doomsday drum
The fear of yet another war to come

A fear that grips and makes you sweat
Your nerves on edge - no breakdown - yet
For if war comes with its horrors anew
That war may leave of us a few

But a few than may start a world that is sane
By loving each other for no selfish gain
Except that all may unite and live in peace
The fear of our forefathers then may cease

Allan Galsworthy

LOVE AT THE FAIR 1954

Loud brash music from rides abound,
      Filling your head with exciting sound.
Tonight's the night you've saved pennies for,
      The dearest ride's a tanner and no more.
Roll-a-penny, keep off the line
      Ball in a bucket, bounce out every time.
Knock off a coconut give it a whirl,
      Try the darts impress your girl.
Hold hands on the Chair-Plane swing out into space,
      Ride the Ghost Train, plant a kiss on your face.
Dodgems, rifles, waltzers too
      Hall of mirrors having a giggle with you.
Candyfloss, Butterkisk, giant lollies to lick
      Hoping the Big Wheel doesn't make you sick.
We know the prizes cost more than their worth,
      But they were tokens of love for the best girl on earth.

John Small

COMMON COLD

There's many a thing we often dread
But there's nothing worse than a cold in the head
A runny nose and a bad sore throat
That makes you talk like a gruff old goat.
The head feels full like a stuffed pillow,
A cough on the chest that sounds like a bellow.
Your eyes keep running and your nose feels so sore,
Blowing your nose with hankies galore.
Your body feels heavy and so does your brain,
Your mouth is all tacky it tastes like a drain.
The sneezing and coughing and blowing your nose,
It makes you feel lousy like nobody knows.
You sniff up Vick or rub it on your chest
Then try to lay down to give your head a rest.
The common cold germs we all really dread
Why do they always attack the head?
Your scalp itches and feels like a wig
When you look in the mirror you look sick as a pig
Your face feels lousy all sticky with sweat
It's amazing where all those little germs get.
After a week or so, and you start to feel fitter,
You'll probably pass it on to some other poor old critter.

Elaine Loche

WARRIOR, CHILD OF GOD

There is no warrior like a child of God,
who carries the shield of faith.
He can fight evil spirits and demons,
with the belt of Truth 'round his waist.

There is no warrior like a child of God
standing firm in any nation.
Wearing the breastplate of Righteousness,
and the helmet of Salvation.

44

There is no warrior like a child of God
against cosmic powers he'll stand,
and challenge the accuser
with the word of God in his hand.

There is no warrior like a child of God
boldly shouting - 'Satan, you lose,'
and marching through Hell's Legions -
with the Gospel of Peace, as his shoes.

John Wallwork

DESPAIR

Sky overcast
Face downcast
A man walks alone
He dreams of his past

Not much money
But jobs to be had
Collieries working
It wasn't so bad

The man looks up
Despair in his eyes
No chance of a job
No clear skies

A ray of sunshine from the sky
A sign of hope, no time to cry
A glint in his eyes as he hurries his pace
A hint of a smile on his careworn face

The sky is blue, there's a new life ahead
He'd show them all
He's not yet dead

Ivy Picton Evans

MOTHER EARTH AND OUR UNIVERSE

This planet Earth is our home
where we live and have our being
her beauty is beyond compare
she gives to us all we need
her gifts of life she shares
in the food, water and the air we breathe
we use her space, her plants, her trees,
so why do we destroy her with our human greed?
Mankind pollutes the atmosphere, the rivers and the seas,
creates holes in the ozone layer
and causes pain and suffering everywhere
but we can change
and turn things round to how it's meant to be
we can learn to give tender loving care to all living things
give respect to life in all its forms
give our love and healing power
to Mother Earth and the Universe
and the future shall be blessed
with peace for all to share

Christina Porritt

MY FRIEND, THE VOLE

Down by the river in a quiet secluded place
Lives my friend the water vole, he has a furry face,
Sharp bright eyes and a short stubby nose.
Heron, owls and pike are a few of his foes.
He is often referred to as a water rat
But do not let him hear, he's offended by that!
Water, in truth, is part of his name
But rat and vole are never the same.
One is a pest and a menace, you'll find
The other, my friend, is the harmless kind!

Jennifer Ashman

HAVE YOU EVER? - A POEM OF NORFOLK

Have you ever walked along a deserted beach,
Making footprints that very soon will be no more,
In between pebbles of every shape and hue?
And watched sanderlings run, like clockwork birds, along the shore,
Whilst up above, the terns hover, then dive for food,
And the ringed plover, camouflaged so well,
Suddenly vanishes from sight amongst the stones,
As you stop to pick up a small pink shell?

Have you ever strolled through a field of poppies,
Or walked a cowslip-bordered country lane?
Listened to the nightjar's evening 'chirring',
Or an April cuckoo telling us it's springtime once again?
Have you seen a long-legged hare race across a field,
Or searched for fungi on an autumn day of gold and red,
Marvelled at the perfume of frothy-headed meadowsweet,
And listened to the yellow-hammer's plea for cheese-less bread?

Have you ever watched, unseen, a tiny muntjac deer,
Or walked through reed beds on an icy winter's day?
Heard the bittern's mournful booming,
Or watched a marsh harrier majestically following its prey?
Have you seen young grebe riding on their mother's back,
Or a motionless heron, fishing, so patiently?
Or watched stripy little shelduck learning how to dive?
It's all out there for anyone to see - all free.

Susan Wooden

THE FLICKERING FIRE

The flickering fire, whose leaping flames,
Conjure up pictures, places and names,
Some long forgotten, others quite new,
Events and occasions, come back into view,
Times that have gone, though still in the mind,
Brought forth once again to unravel, unwind,
Emotions rekindled, once were thought dead,
Relived and remembered, words lovingly said,
Meetings recounted, embraces held dear,
Intimate phrases, words of good cheer,
Moments so fleeting, all in the past,
Cherished forever, years gone so fast,
Shall not be forgotten, while memories live,
And flames keep on dancing, and help us to give,
A smile on reflection, a moment's desire,
This time of contentment, this warm cosy fire.

Andrew Quinn

MEMORIES

There she stands in skin tight jeans,
A replica of what I had been.
Slim and beautiful with hair of gold,
What a shame I'm getting old.

Youth flashes by like a flash of light,
All we have left are lonely nights.
The photo album is a source of joy,
All my memories of my girl and boy.

From babe-in-arms to wedding day,
There's nothing more for me to say.
Just close my eyes and dream again
That the boy is eight and the girl is ten.

L B Yates

AUTUMN

Autumn how I despise you,
I find no comfort in your russet hue,
Renewed again are my feelings of dire dismay,
As you bring to me the aroma of decay.

No! I cannot see the long sleep you bring,
As essential to plants' re-birth in spring,
My eyes are offended by the dead and dying,
You murdered summer, there's no denying.

I've tried to see beauty in your distinctive gown,
Of orange and red and shades of brown,
But always as always my heart does dwell,
Not on your dress, but death's bitter sweet smell.

Every year the self same crime,
You come to murder summertime,
For this I cannot forgive you - ever,
To love you? No never *never!*

Rita B Armitage

CROW

I summon you Crow
With my bare knuckle to glass
And framed with ludicrous exposure -
I hang my head in envy.

Will you remember my face from that
Crazy window?
Do you know you are free?
In the sky you reign
Far below I remain
While into the clouds you calmly fly.

C Bain

INKY-WOO

There was a man called Inky-woo
Whose favourite food was kangaroo.
He walked for miles on legs so thin,
With arms so long and a pointed chin.
He wore a hat that he'd made of grass
And his eyes stood out like bottle glass.
There was a man called Inky-woo;
A wild man some said - perhaps that's true.
But wild or not, the tales he told
Would hold you spellbound young or old.
Tales of lands across the seas,
Tales of monster sharks and fleas.
There was this man called Inky-woo
Whose age, he claimed, was ninety-two.
No wife he had, or so he said,
For he wouldn't sleep on a double bed.
At night he talked to toads and mice
And fed them all on bowls of rice.
So when you think you're feeling blue,
Just spare a thought for Inky-woo.

Richard Newton

UNTITLED

A darkened room, the candle extinguished.
An eternal silence, in a world where feelings pass unspoken.
Hands reach out to touch, grabbing parcels of emptiness.
Tears fall and dry, ignored.
Screaming souls yearn to be heard.
An awareness of others, ripens as the forbidden fruit.
Longing to be part of anything good.
Freedom does not exist, only a caged heart.
Welcome to my world.

Lucy Woollard

A DOG'S LIFE

In the depths of winter on this
   Long December night
Listening to the sound of the
   Cold icy sleet rapping at
   Our window, as I lay at my
Master's rested slippered feet
   Sleepily staring into the
Glowing embered fire, its red
Flames sending shadows
   Dancing round our softly
Lit room
The clock with its restful ticking
   Is the only sound
Or maybe the odd bark outside
From an irritant hound
   I've been for my walk and
Done all the rest, have had my
Light supper, which I ate with great
   Zest. A dog's life so they say
Well I wouldn't swap mine any day.

Christine Corbett

OCCASION

Confused confused did you say? No no not I - I might on occasion
Call you another name but then I meet a lot of people in my game.
I remember one day I was called to address a meeting at the town hall
To talk about gardening for all,
A man introduced me as Mr Smythe, 'No I said Mr Smith's my name,'
I started my talk but giggles put me to shame,
I found I was in a meeting that had no bearing on my speaking
Naturist a way of life, 'Excuse me,' I said and turned my back and fled.

Graham Hodgkins

LOVE ME FOREVER

These words that I write
are for your eyes alone.
Give me your love forever,
for I will give you all
that I hold.
All my todays and tomorrows
belong to you alone,
I will love you forever
this man that you are.
You are my north, south
my east and my west.
Put a hat on the sun,
give me shades for my eyes.
You have made me sparkle,
I light up when I
see your beautiful eyes.
Give me all your love
forever.
Not for just a day,
but for all eternity.

Kathleen Scarborough

STALLED

Without you I'm empty,
No petrol, no fuel,
My engine won't start,
The brakes are on full.

Pain punctures my tyres,
Releasing all air,
This body has nothing,
Without you there.

Julie McKerchar

COLOUR ME FREE

Paint me a slice of blue wilderness sky,
Tucked behind mountain peaks purple and grey,
From whence the green pine forests march to the shore
Of the shimmering lake at my feet.

Colour me natural, blend me in well.
Draw me a breath of the sweetest of air.
Fill up my heart with the longing to dwell
In perpetual harmony there.

Where freedom is colourless, boundless and fair
No living creature controls the domain
Of Nature, Earth's matriarch, whose loving care
Pervades the rugged terrain.

Blend me in with the back-cloth of seasons that change.
In chameleon colours my attitudes dress,
So I may be one with the land, and arrange
That my shadow's all I possess.

Let cool mountain streams trickle over my feet.
Head in the clouds I will sit there and dream
Of times when the winning was really defeat,
And losing was part of the scheme.

Let me soar with the eagle across the divide,
Swim with the otters and fish in the lakes,
Run with the deer to the forest to hide
From civilisation's mistakes.

Alex Forbes

INFORMATION SUPERHIGHWAY BLUES

Across a crowded computer room
Big Ram's cursor flashing green,
He was hoping once more to interface
With the operator of his dreams.

But she backspaced his ardour.
Downloaded his lovedrive too.
'No more hard disc Big Ram,' she mused.
'It's a floppy one for you.'

He was flush right and justified,
He put his mouse away.
Had she erased from her directory
The computer games they used to play?

Just because she had a new laptop
She spoke his font no more,
And was giving Big Ram a boot up
The joystick out the door.

Now she ran with the worldly crowd,
Surfed the net with that motley crew
In the superhighway's singles bar,
Making love on the VDU.

There was no key to retrieve his love.
Her gain was Big Ram's loss.
So he'd have to save his bite sized passion
And exit once more to dos.

David Boyle

MY BED

The radio comes on
I awake from my sleep
It's the break of the dawn
The birds start to cheep

Another night over
Another day ahead
Oh how I'll look forward
To get back to my bed

My eyes aren't quite open
I'm too tired to speak
The children are calling
But still in bare feet

I'm way behind time
Oh I hate this rush
Instead of the dawn
I wish it was dusk

I promise myself
I'll get more organised
So that this time tomorrow
I won't have to rise

A few minutes more
Not moving a muscle
Enjoying the luxury
Before the hustle and bustle

I thank God for good health
And the things He has made
But most of all
I thank God for my bed.

Noelle McLaren

HAIR TODAY . . .

When I was born I didn't have a hair upon my head,
But as the weeks went by I grew some downy stuff instead.
It started to grow thicker and in fact it turned quite black.
But then my little pillow wore a bald spot at the back.

My follicles worked overtime and soon my flowing mane
Looked beautiful - until the barber cut if off again.
In all my early years at school, despite every attempt
To master it with brush and comb, my hair remained unkempt.

But throughout all my teenage years it was a different story.
With Brylcreamed waves and sideburns it became my crowing glory.
Then, looking in a mirror, I was very shocked indeed;
My hairline took me by surprise and started to recede.

I married and had children and the years just slipped away
And, almost imperceptibly, the black hair turned to grey.
When looking at old photographs my grandchildren all stare.
They've never seen their grandpa with such dark and wavy hair.

What hair remains upon my head is very widely parted,
In fact if I lose any more I'm right back where I started.
I've joined the ranks of bearded men with hair upon their faces.
I don't admit to being bald; the hairs have just changed places!

Dennis Turner

A SOLDIER

A soldier dressed all in green,
Is most definitely a sight to be seen.
His rifle clutched close to his chest,
Trying to be better than the rest.

His boots and rifle shining bright,
And straight ahead is his sight.
His thoughts going to a girl he's missing,
And can't wait till her doorbell he's ringing.

56

The beautiful girl all alone,
Walking through her empty home.
Her thoughts on her absent soldier,
Wishing he was here to hold her.

They sit looking up to the same sky,
And in the stars she can see his twinkling eye.
They dream of their lover far away,
But they will be together, some day.

Philip Bettinson

MISTER CHASPER

Mister Chasper the chimp had an arm that was limp
which he noticed as he swung through the trees.
When he'd stretch to the right
for the first branch in sight,
he'd tumble right down and land on his knees.

But he'd quickly regain his hind legs just the same,
to start swinging as if nothing had failed.
Every morning he'd fly
from the lamp posts up high
in his yellow top hat, bow tie and tails.

With his ups and his downs from the sky to the ground,
he never showed an ounce of self-pity
as he made his way home
to the Upper Malone
from the Bank where he worked in the city.

He was a welcome sight both by day and by night,
and he'd a greeting for all as he passed.
With his wave and a smile,
he made living worthwhile,
this amazing little gent from Belfast.

Robert E Corrigan

LOST FOR EVER

The farms of my childhood
Have long since gone,
With big horses and wagons,
And ploughman 'John'.
Orchards of apples,
Plums damsons and pears,
Fields and barns that we played in
Without any cares.
We saw wild things shot,
And the fat pigs killed,
We saw newly born creatures,
And the rich earth tilled.
Milk was squirted from cows
By hand twice a day,
And the hens all decided
Where they wished to lay.
We watched greedy piglets
Suckled by their mum
And wondered so many
Had grown in her tum.
We loved Yorkshire puddings
Cooked under roast beef,
We had pigeon and rabbit
And rook pies to eat.
Now lost for ever
To more modern ways,
I shall always remember
My past childhood days.

Joan Hancock

THE TAXI

As it weaves its way from east to south,
'long country roads to harbour town.
The pain of separation engulfs my weary mind.

Your life was planned, you said,
but in you stepped to mine . . . so gently.

Why did you stop to smell the roses on the way,
instead of passing through?

But stop you did.

And now our lives can never be the same again.

Our struggling hearts, so knowledgeable of the depth
of love which exists
Tear us hourly, limb by limb, as both we try to
live as other wish.

This eve, as you will walk Vespucci's Shores a
different fantasy, from that which often haunts
your troubled soul.
I feel this sadness, so deeply rooted in our lives
and pray one day you will return to truth.

Anne Davis

NEED IN EXILE

And as she walked behind her husband
Sainsbury carrier bag, mouth packed with *paan*
Her mind put to gossip caste rites
And the horrible price of Basmati rice

It began to snow.

Surprised, she tongued her *paan* to one cheek
And followed her husband around a corner street,

Kaush

A RHETORICAL DREAM

Pale orbit,
      Blackened by eerie silhouettes.
A lone cloud slips motionlessly by
As the dark skies descend
The world dances to a whole new tune
The glittering lights
      Of the celestial haunt.
Our trip begins.

Distorted shapes and dancing lights
      Betray true clarity
Crooked heights hold no fear
As this is an old acquaintance, my friend.

We feel no pain
      In the labyrinth of our minds
But beware the unknown challenge
As it is a proficient killer
And you will lose . . .
. . . sleep.

David McManus

MY MUMMY

My mummy is so funny
She has a big fat tummy
It wobbles when she walks

She has more fat than a chip shop fryer

Great big drawers tied with string
She is not worried at being fat
She was made that way so that's that

When my mates laugh
At my mum's size

I turn and say she has got more
To love me with so there

Then holding mummy's hand
We walk away without a care.

Melfyn Dean

SLEEPLESS NIGHTS

Why when I lie with my eyes clenched shut
and my only wish for sleep,
does my mind go whizzing round and round
as I lie here counting sheep?

Why do I toss and turn so long
as the clock ticks slowly on,
when all I want is a gentle snore
and a peaceful sleep till dawn?

The land of nod seems so far away
as I lie here in the dark,
with the late night sounds and the taxi roar
and even a distant bark.

Oh for an hour in the land of dreams
with my troubles all forgot,
but it's not to be, as all I hear
is the ticking of the clock.

And now the morning light seeps in
and daylight sounds I hear,
I sit up rigid, what's that noise?
The alarm bell's in my ear.

Joy Gray

UNREALISED GOALS

Remember this LA woman
Driving in your car
The untouchables, no-one could reach us with sensibility or constraint
Four years down the line
I wish I could unlearn what I have
Just to keep the audacity, the innocence.
We were going to be Rock 'n' Roll stars
Then. Now I want a job
To buy a house to rear the kids
I wait to bear.
Then as long as the petrol tank was full
We had our freedom, immune to everything except us
And what we wanted to do.
Anything was possible
Now we're just ordinary riders on this storm.
If the rat race doesn't get us, old age will.

Kirsty Oliver

ROMANIA REVISITED: LANGUAGE TEACHING

Like a conjurer I stood at the front.
'Now for my first trick,' with books
And bag, chairs, pencils, pens.
Or an entertainer, 'Simon says.'
Or just an idiot, the smallest barely
Able to write, the oldest always wrong.
I had to laugh: they were so good
They redeemed for me those nightmare
Days at my first teaching post -
Portia meaningless among the desks.
Here, in this basement, on wooden benches.
They said goodbye and thanks with flowers,
And glass, pottery, cards in Polish.

David Barratt

ONE BREATH

I watch you sleeping,
heart beating,
hair hiding your cheek.
Eyes fastened close,
nobody knows,
the answers you seek.
Chest rising and falling.
We're stalling
by using a machine
I don't want you gone
but your time to move on
has already come and been.

The sound that you make
with each breath you take
lies hollow in my ears.
And your legacy left
will be the sound of that breath
will be the sound of that breath
will be the sound of that breath . . .

Zowie Hay

FIELD MOUSE

When darkness falls,
And children sleep,
Out from its hole the mouse will creep.
Scampering across the grassy ground,
It hopes that it will not be found.
But up up high upon a branch,
A nasty owl saw his chance.
He swooped down low
And caught the mouse,
And took him to his comfy house.

Lauren Stanley (9)

63

THE WEEPING HOUSE

Weeds in the gravel silenced the car tyres,
And then the confidence of our footsteps.
The house waited patiently for our approach,
Perhaps asleep, its shuttered eyes closed.
Shrubbery to both sides, overgrown, menacing green,
Crowded any visitors into the front porch.
Inside, a litter of junk mail, dark with footprints,
Date stamped over years, sprawled by the door.
Cold as a tomb, peeling walls, leaning banisters,
And stained bathrooms greeted us with bills.
Once gracious rooms pleaded for care, offering,
Shelter and love in exchange. But for what effort, time,
Expense. No. Then regretfully, again No.
Outside, trying to get warm, as we left,
Looking back, we saw the oddest effect.
Rust from shutter bolts, traced red-brown tear tracks.
The house was weeping, soundlessly, hopelessly.

Howard Baker

MY WIFE

I remember the seconds
of the first day we met.
My heart knew from those
moments our future was set.

You are to me the stars in
the sky. Without the warmth
of your love I'd wither and die.

So three words being 'I love you'
for my beautiful wife.
I'll love you forever to the
end of my life.

Michael Keszeg

THE FORGOTTEN ONES

See how the children play in the sands.
See how they cry with outstretched hands.
See how they wander in lonely despair.
See how they sit with their vacant stare.
See how they crawl in the dust and the dirt.
See how they have no shoes and no shirt.
See how they live in squalor and pain.
See how they pray for life-giving rain.

Look at our money, our riches and wealth.
Look at the west its fortune and health.
Look at our mountains of butter and grain.
Look at our excuses, they're poor and they're lame.
Look at our reasons for not helping their plight.
Look at us safe in our beds at night.
Look at our selfishness and our greed.
Look at our gadgets and trinkets: our 'material' need.

For them another day of living in fear.
For them another day becomes another year.
For them another child born into this.
For them another life for the world to dismiss.
For them another day with no end in sight.
For them another day and endless night.
For them another day of torment; trouble; strife.
For them another day of their hell called life.

Elizabeth Basham

WHAT SHALL WE DO IF . . . ?

What shall we do if,
Crusty Auntie Ethel gets kidnapped?
Have a party, obviously.
What shall we do if,
The world crashes into Mars?
Explore Mars, obviously,
What shall we do if,
The computer blows up?
Get a new computer, obviously.
What shall we do if,
Manchester United loses 10-0 to Birmingham?
Faint in shock, obviously.
What shall we do if,
Every milkman goes on strike?
Buy a cow, obviously.
And what shall we do if,
The author of this poem doesn't want to stop writing?
Tell her to shut up and nick her pen, obviously!

Vicky Westgate

WHY?

Mummy, I want to ask you a question,
Will you promise to answer me?
Why haven't I got wings like a bird to fly?
And, what does the Queen have for tea?

Why is the table so big and high?
And why are you and Daddy so tall?
Will I grow to be big one day
Or will I always be this small?

And.,why is an orange round Mummy?
Why can't it be green or blue?
Why are snakes all slithery
I don't like them much, do you?

What does Jesus *do* in Heaven?
Can He play with train sets and things?
Or does He have to sit around all day,
And talk to all them Angels and Kings?

Mary Paton

A DEAD CERT

How the horse amazes
With king like posture
Heraldic graces.

Imperial ramble, gentle canter
Emerald banquet, shrewd supplanter.

How the horse surprises
With queen like elegance
Docile disguises.

Omnipotent amble, phlegmatic stare
Incisive reason, exalted prayer.

How the horse astounds
With prince like nobility
Sovereign uncrowned.

But

As man chastises, with race-card fervour
The wilful beast, pro tem observer

The graceful ebb, royal recision
Disintegrate in jet-like vision

The beast will turn, regent disown
With serf-like vengeance, claim his throne.

Ashley Borrett

MOON

Eleven thirty four

The wag of a dog

The man in the moon.

Desperate for bloodied steak and alcohol,
I half ran, half staggered, the night so
cruel and merciless.

- St James' Park from the pulsating facades
of the dirty streets, my breath a foul fog on
the air. Yellow stained incisors - growing.

The sanctum of the undergrowth, deep dig the icy
fingers into my mind, blinding pain at the base
of my spine, wrenching into distorted animation.
Screams of agony, tearing the cloth,
metamorphosis of skeletal composure under bristling
fur.

Rank the smells, choking, retching. Tortured whimpers,
barking, howling, cursing . . . the man in the moon.

Eleven forty four.

The wag of a dog,

the girl in the park.

- The sweet tantalising aromas a technicoloured
explosion of blinding light. Deep arousal, can't
control, the sweet flesh moving closer.

Ancient predatory instincts, stalking, hackles raised.
Salivary juices flowing over sharpened points.
The sweet, sweet scent of ivory skin in the moonlight,
chanting demons, passions rising and . . . Oh!
How much I would have her know.

Eleven fifty four.

The wag of a dog,

with crimson stained lips . . .

Anthony Graham

AN ARGUMENTATIVE LAD

I have an awful problem
I'm always talking back.
If I was in employment
I sure would get the sack.
But I am quite determined
To say what I think's right
Even if that means I
Stay up to twelve at night.
Just to have the last word
And make my folks real mad.
Aren't they so lucky
To have an argumentative lad?
There are some kids who never
Speak up for their own rights
I say to them you suckers
You foolish little mites.
Speak up and keep on answering back
That's what us kids must do
If you don't take my strong advice
One day you're sure to rue.
I'm not a nasty fellow
I really am quite sweet,
Come along and see me
A charming chap you'll meet.

Olive C Blair

MY PRAYER

In my hour of darkness
be my light.
When I am hungry
be my food.
If I get lost
guide me to the right road.
When I feel lonely
become my companion.
If I have a problem
help me to solve it.
When I become cold
give me warmth.
In my moments of weakness
supply me with strength.
But above all else Lord,
I ask this of You,
now that the door of my
heart is open,
enter it.

Maggie Prickett

THE LITTLE ROBIN

I see a little robin sitting there,
I love to see him anywhere.
I watch him for hours and hours,
Sitting in between the flowers.
He comes up to me,
For now he is free.
He sings to me,
High up in the tree.
He flies north, east, south and west,
God bless the little robin for he deserves the best.

Anouska Aitkenhead

WHEN DREAMS TRESPASS

One night
I dreamt I lay my head on your shoulder

Not in a sensuous way
nor as a calming sequel to reckless passion

But with careless familiarity
as if I were well used to loving you.

Then,
for a moment,
I placed the palm of my hand on your upper arm
and you abstractly accepted this casual gesture
so that I knew our closeness was long established
requiring no further consideration.

And I could see,
through the window of my dream,
other daytime faces
talking and laughing with impersonal disregard.

It seemed they too recognised our random ways
like head on shoulder
and private words
And, with quiet disinterest, nodded at our attachment.

Yet today,
You move about the office importantly
Dealing singlemindedly with the commonplace,
Strangely oblivious to the bewildering night shift in our emotions.
I pass you a 'phone message
Stark black ink on yellow paper
Unflinchingly, our hands brush.
And with a whisper of regret . . .
 . . . I thank God.

Victoria Moores

PLEASE CALL LATER

It sits in the corner ready for action
You'd call it useful, not an attraction.
It's ready to ring to bring you the call
Whether standing on the side or hung on the wall.
The colours are varied but mine is black
The cord has been pulled and now it hangs slack
I'll take a chance with a cordless on trial
To think where I'd use it would cause me to smile
It could make you wonder when I'm talking to you
I'll give you no hint, suggestion or clue
If you phone for a chat and my words are few
The parachute's open and the ground's in view
I'll ring you back when on safer ground
My head just now is spinning round.
This hospital's nice, no complaints at all
If only the phone wasn't down the hall
A mobile would be nice with a leg in plaster
But a mobile for me was just a disaster.

V Campbell

CHESTNUT LEAVES

The wind came in during the night
bearing shards of raw rain
and stripped the trees of their leaves;
they lie like storm-tossed gondolas
on the floor of the forest,
anchored by pools of clear water;
their colour of sere-veined hands,
upturned to the morning's light,
gently lifting on a light swell,
breath burnishing a new day.

Richard A Farrow

JOHN

I wish I'd met the Mam he knew
The dad that watched him as he grew
Into the man, I later met
Much older now l know, and yet

I wish I'd held his hand when small
As brothers do, for fear he'd fall
And through the games that children play
Build memories, amiss, today

I envy all the friends he had
That stuck by him, through good, and bad
Those tales they tell, of bygone years
So sadly fill my eyes with tears.

Except for flesh and blood, you see
We lived our lives independently
Though chance, we had to put this right
Too hard, too late, to re-unite

Until too late the good Lord took
My brother John, and closed the book
The lesson that I've learnt I fear
Is life's too short, for those held dear

It's shorter still, if they don't know
Because you've failed to tell them so
So open up your hearts to kin
Don't harbour pain so deep within

For once you've gone, this earth you've left
And kin, you leave behind
Memories, are all that's left
To ease, an ever anxious mind.

Roy Wyatt

ALONE

Darkness fills the evening air
As I walk by they watch and stare

Only I can feel the cold
Stories of me that they've been told

I am alone without a friend
No hope of a hand that they might lend

No one to care if I'm tired or ill
No warm house fire to ease the chill

I have no house; I have no home
Left outside like a garden gnome

As I walk down the lonely street
I see a poor child being struck and beat

As I look at things that are surrounding me
And remember how life used to be

As I hold my whiskey bottle tight
I see the sky turn brilliant white

As the tunnel end grows near
The sound of weeping, a flood of tears

None of them ever really cared
All they want is my money to share.

Stacey Hempshall (15)

FARMING WITH HORSES

When harvest is finished, the horse ploughs begin
Turning over fleet furrows, grass neatly turned in.
Now thousands of spiders spin their long silky threads,
Catching dew of early morning, as we rise from our beds.
Along come the seed harrows, this fine array to spoil.
While drill follows after, sowing seeds in the soil
To grow, and to flourish, for harvest next year
With the hope of a profit, which could disappear.

Two horses are plodding between rows of sugar beet,
Pulling bow plough, to leave beet raised very neat.
People with their backs bent, now sweating with toil,
Leaving neat rows behind them, when removing the soil.
Then later with billhook, and skill of the strike,
Beheads them, and leaves beet in heaps, all alike
To be forked onto tumbril, pulled by a carthorse.
Now taken to station, to load on rail trucks of course.

Spring has arrived now, with the warmth of the sun,
The cattle go grazing, calves have their first run.
There's meadows to fertilise, winter corns to top-dress.
There's spring barley to sow, behind harrows and press.
Baulks for the potatoes, baulks for mangolds as well.
The horses kept busy, on what job? Who can tell?
We must chain-harrow meadows, followed by rolls,
They are always unlevel, due to frosts and the moles.

Now on with the harvest, for August is here,
The corn is now golden, with bent over ear.
Go get the self-binder, some neat sheaves to make.
Three horses now tiring, plus three fresh for the break.
Three people now busy, making shocks in a row,
Picking two rows of sheaves each this, each one will know.
Now load up the wagons, with sheaves, ears looking in,
To be stacked in the stackyard, who says we won't win?

W G Frosdick

THE MORNING AFTER THE NIGHT BEFORE

Oh why do I do it? I really don't know,
I knew it wouldn't last, that lovely rosy glow,
It's left me with a head so full of pain,
And my whole body feeling drained,
'Just one more,' that's all I said,
Then I must be home to bed,
But now that morning's come I've found,
My great big bed is still going round,
A glass of water I must take,
Before I completely dehydrate!
Why do liver salts fizz so loud?
And to swallow a pill I've just found,
There's no way that they'll go down,
Not while your head is swimming around.
Next time I go out . . . if I'm asked,
On spirits and wine I must say pass,
And stick to fruit juice or a coke,
'Cos drinking too much is no joke!

Chrissie Martin

AFFAIRS OF THE HEART

He said she had a twisted mind.
Suspicions fuelled by guilty looks,
Conclusions drawn from clues left behind,
Searched for in pockets and hidden nooks.

Not wanting to face the truth
Hoping it will run its course,
But compelled to seek out proof
Wanting to fill him with remorse.

Blaming herself - feelings taken for granted
Desperate now to win him back
When was this sprouting seed planted?
Or is he just following the pack?

She thought he was different from the rest
- Thought she was different too,
Issues ignored instead of addressed
Words unspoken, thoughts too few.

R Langridge

WINTERTIME

Slowly, lazily, twisting, twirling falling snowflakes dance and play,
hypnotising, mesmerising lonely travellers on their way.

Drifting up against the hedges, filling ditches, cloaking all,
with a mantle white and glistening settling on the garden wall.

Decorating house and cottage, powdering the bleak bare tree,
little children laughing gaily slip and slide home for their tea.

Cars abandoned in the snow drifts, birds fly by on frozen wing,
searching for the little cake crumbs, searching with no time to sing.

Ice coated ponds and frozen puddles, snow covered fences row on row,
tingling toes and tingling fingers, red cheeks and noses all aglow.
Snowploughs clear the blocked up roadway, footprints trailing up the path,
cosy rooms with windows curtained, crackling log fires in the hearth.

So the world of Mother Nature, silent, still, lies fast asleep,
beneath its cold, white ermine raiment beneath the snow so crisp and deep.

Pamela Eckhardt

REFLECTIONS

I looked in a mirror when I was a child, the face that I saw looked back
and smiled.
An innocent wonder was what I could see - the experience of life was
beckoning me.

Later I looked in the mirror once more, I still can remember the
image I saw.
The hair was untidy, the tie wasn't straight. Play was important and
'living' could wait.

And then, once again, after many more years, I look in the mirror -
a young man appears
The eyes are still smiling, the chin growing dark. The passage of time
leaving its mark.

By now this same mirror is constantly used, the young man reflected is
mostly amused.
His hair style is different - he follows the trend. Life is exciting, where
will it end?

More years have gone by and the mirror has grown, it's used by his wife
and the 'seed' he has sown.
Though the eyes are still smiling the face has grown wise, The young man
is seen in a different guise.

Then comes the day when he sees, with surprise, that the sparkle he knew -
has gone from his eyes.
The hair, which hung down in a haphazard way is suddenly orderly,
thinner and grey.

The young man is old now and looks at the wall. The mirror which hangs
there is not used at all.
His experience of life has not been too kind. He keeps his reflections
locked in his mind.

Gerry Steele

PLAYTIME

They did not think
Little pigs all sweet and pink
Their play would have to end
As they are made to spend
All day in silent gloom
With little or no room
To turn and twist and run
To leap about in playful fun
In stiff painful rows they wait
For master coming in the gate
Will he never come
To let them gallop in the sun?
They may not have a pretty face
But they can comprehend
The loathsome fate, the dreadful end.
While man waits with knife and fork
For he must have his joint of pork.

Benna Smith

DID I STIR YOU?

Did I stir you?
Steal you from stagnant slumber
Caress your cancer with emotion's knife
Have I tamed you?
Domesticated you by demand not pleads
With orders instead of famed request
Can I greet you?
Bearing our twin burden of anticipation
A sour scent to repel danger from your mind
Will we make amends?
To heal rifts and build bridges
To fill oceans and a new canvas

Giles Milner

I'VE FOUND LOVE!

Like a fresh breath of air,
My heart skips a beat,
Alone no more,
For I am complete.

The spark in my heart,
Has burst into flame,
Love feeds the hunger,
No more sorrow or pain.

Human bond of eternity
Runs deep into my soul
My feelings are clear
Life has just begun.

Clare Dunn

PROUD FATHER

Hoist up the flags, raise the banners high,
Put festoon and bunting right up to the sky,
Tell amateur dramatics to set up the stage,
Ring up the editor to hold the front page,
Parade out the marching band with trumpet and horn,
Set the town crier proclaiming, A Baby Is Born,
Send faxes and telegrams, roses and wine,
Parent and offspring are both doing fine,
Ferry close relations to visit and see
Tired Mother, proud Father and new family.
Nine months have I waited to look on the face
Of my immortality surround by lace,
My heart is voluptuously filled with delight,
So set off the fireworks and light up the night.

D T Morgan

DAD

Always there to comfort me
A soft and gentle man
You always know just what I need
You help me if you can
You never moan complaints are few
But deep inside you're hurting too
You keep it in you won't let go
The pain you feel, you never show
You hide it to protect us all
A man you stand, you never fall
You've cared for me, I love you so
I never want to let you go
You're strong although you're fading fast
You're all for the future
Never the past
Always for others in your mind
A lovely man your heart so kind
And now you've got to go away
Your time has come you cannot stay
But if I had one wish come true
I'd wish that I could be with you
When you're no longer here with me
I'll miss you until eternity
The gentle smile, the friendly face
No one will ever take your place
I love you Dad.

Vanessa Ball

SIGHTS AND SOUNDS

Way up high a nightingale sings.
Somewhere in the valley a church bell rings.
A blackbird sings his song of love.
And the trees reach up to the sky above.
Where their leaves are kissed by a gentle breeze
That is blowing softly through the trees.
The sun shines down from a cloudless sky,
And a dragon-fly flits slowly by.
The sun reflects on gossamer wings.
And still up high a nightingale sings,
Singing his song that is just for me
As I sit beneath the old oak tree.
Dreaming as the world goes by,
Of the trees, the grass, the sun, the sky.
I see the tiny spider's webs,
Lovingly made with silken threads.
They glitter in the morning light
Like a thousand diamonds shining bright.
I love this place where all seems free,
And I really love this old oak tree
Beneath whose branches I sit and dream,
Lulled by the music of the tiny stream
As it passes by the old oak tree,
On its way to the open sea.

A F J Wakeford

BLUE ANGELS

They say angels are found only in heaven,
But I know that this is not so,
There are also angels down on earth,
As well we all know.

They are courteous, kind and gentle,
Dressed in a lovely blue.
Always a smile and a kind word,
When you think your world is through.

They have the knack of saying,
The right thing to ease the pain,
Clarify the situation,
To help clear a puzzled brain.

Their skill and dedication,
When we think there is little hope,
The words and how they say them,
Make it easier to cope.

So when life's chapter is over,
And we come to chapter two,
Angels above won't be dressed in white,
They will all be dressed in blue.

Words of gratitude, where do I really start?
But thank you is a very large word,
When spoken from the heart.
Thank you.

Dennis Bowern

THE DIFFERENT GIFT

It's a gift for which, so many long.
For silvery phrases from one's tongue.
To hold them rapt when in debate,
Of any consequence and weight.

To put one's views and thoughts by merely,
One sharp sentence stated clearly.
Cutting words that like an asp's sting,
Leaves your enemy smarting gasping.

But a gift for song is one not shared,
By many of these common herd.
This gift strikes chords in a listener's heart,
Helps each one to play their part.

It melts within and soothes the pains,
Of any anger that remains.
Takes you back to happy times.
Lifts you up in lilting rhymes.

Has been known to make men weep.
Helps your baby go to sleep.
Makes youth dance and laugh and cry.
Makes old men dream and lovers sigh.

P Day

REALMS OF NATURE

Green belt is my neighbour
And fortunately for me
My small house has large windows
Enabling me to see,

The glory of changing seasons,
And, so many wildlife friends
Busy with various duties
On which survival depends.

84

A heron flying in to land
Is a highlight of my day
It doesn't stay long, just stands awhile
Then is up off and away.

Within the realms of nature
Each and all have a place
As keepers of God given beauty
This wondrous world to grace.

Amelia Canning

AN APE COILED IN A WINDING SHEET

Maudlin dreams, a cerecloth wrap
A dead Pharaoh's silent musings
Of inspired lands and mystical kingdoms
A mortal empire of intimate dread
Utopian of a myriad God
Where warriors bleed Elysium thoughts
Sighing under heavy sanguine axes
And over centuries wafts balmy incense
An opium caress for a Stygian shore
Grey and sombre, in a beloved's wake
With a glimmer of a God in a man's eye
A creator created by an Oedipus breed
Ape scholars perform divine autopsies
And a Lord lays cold on a surgical table
Dissected by the species of man
A science of Nietzsche's Zarathustra
Epitaphs of theology by human hand
Carved by primates of wise descent
Who ponder God's enigma
Where weeping angels caress twisting pale bodies
In soft Icarus wings of sorrow
Embalming wax corpses in mysterious dreams
As a truth unfolds in silent splendour

N Sturman

THE AGONY OF WAR

As the shadows lengthen over the trench
Rotting bodies fester an awful stench
The day's merciless conflict's at an end
Will the night bring the enemy to fend?

The horror and futility of war,
How many will die, not knowing what for?
Defeat or victory, fate will decide.
What keeps us going? It's simply sheer pride.

Today the sun's rays shimmered the French air
Oh! For rain-drops to cool my grubby face.
Where are the politicians? It's so unfair.
Please before winter, against time do race.

War brings both physical and mental pain
We lose a few yards, only to regain.
Is there a rifle bullet that bears my name?
Will I be brave and gain eternal fame?

We are but a pawn in a game of chess
Will they ever sort out this bloody mess?
Spare a thought for loved ones so far away.
My Christian faith is tested, but still I pray.

Gwyndaf Williams

UNREQUITED

I need to find a haven of peace where I will find,
Where all my thoughts will flourish and words with time express.
There's something that I need so bad
Sweet love and tenderness.

From all that now awaits me
To aggrieve my aching heart
Whose lonely darkness haunts me
What was complete doth now depart.

Nor search my soul and wonder
And ponder on that place
Where souls entwine forever,
Now elusive without a trace.

The endless yearn of wanting
And always without you
Fills all my sense of passion
Light never shining through.

Dawn Austwick

PARENTAL TRAINING COLLEGE

Why is it your parents can't help nagging you,
Maybe it's what they've been trained to do?
You get in from school and it's 'Why are you late?'
'The bus didn't come so I had to wait.'

The next morning it's close to all out war,
My parents are both so hard to ignore,
I reckon there's a college where parents go,
Where they learn how to nag, annoy and say 'No!'

When you ask to go out the answer is 'Where?'
I don't even think that they really care,
Do you think that they learnt at a special place,
And they learn how to deal with every case?

When I'm a parent I won't do that,
I'll offer 'em sweets and make them fat!
I'll skip classes at that training place,
And I won't dress my children in pretty lace.

When I'm a parent, I'll be really nice,
When they ask to go out, I won't think twice,
When I'm a parent, I won't lay down any laws,
When I'm a parent, I'll ignore all the chores!

Danielle Morey (14)

DAVID'S DREAM

One day while David was walking,
He heard soft voices talking.
'Come with us, it's your lucky day,'
Said two little robins who stood in his way.

'You will see such a wonderful land,'
Said the robins, perched one on each hand.
'A land where all your dreams come true,
It's waiting up there just for you.'

Gently they lifted David up high,
Over the tree-tops and into the sky.
Through the clouds all fluffy and white,
The trees below were soon out of sight.

In the distance he could clearly see,
A land that filled his heart with glee.
Big, juicy strawberries carpet the floor,
With bananas growing by the score.

With feet now firmly on the ground,
Paradise stood there all around.
Lemonade fountains and huge custard lakes,
Bushes covered with cream-filled cakes.

A marshmallow castle stood high on a hill,
Bluebirds sang and flamingos stood still.
Eating and drinking all day long,
David was singing a happy song.

Goblins, gnomes and fairies at play,
While David by the lake did lay.
Bananas dipped in the custard lake,
Arm outstretched for another cream cake.

Then suddenly came a ringing sound,
And David sleepily came around.
Are things always what they seem?
Or had his day been just a dream?

Martyn Mason

ODE TO THE BARD

Handsome raffin excise lad
Wi' the darkest deevilish e'en
Rabbie - ye rule in Scotland
The best - that's iver been

Poetry - it knew fortune
Nae langer - wis it blurred
For - mony a hert - it gleddened
An' mony - it also spurred

Ma distant dream - dear Rabbie
Is tae be - a bit like you
Oh! Rabbie Burns - the wunner
Yer banter - inspires - an' woos

An' if this nicht -
God bless ye
Ye are in some 'higher' sphere
Whaur the licht - is bricht an' shinin'
Look fondly - doon by here

See me! - a learnin' poet
Though no' a maister -
Shair - a fan
Wha' wid dedicate - this sonnet
Tae Rabbie Burns -
The Bard - an' man.

Irene Gunnion

THAT'S JAZZ

To make the Beiderbecke connection
I search through my small collection,
Of Ellington and Holiday
I save the best for Saturday.
Charlie Parker, John Coltrane
Miles Davies I'll play over again.
Bossa Nova with Stan Getz,
Benny Goodman sweetly next.
King Oliver's blues goes on and on
The brilliant Louis Armstrong,
Dizzy Gillespie, Thelonius Monk,
Some think it just a load of junk.
Memories of my misspent youth
From shop to shop and music booth.
Coleman Hawkins tenor sax,
And later days with Fleetwood Macs.
I feel the joy that this sound has
That velvet sound known as . . . *jazz.*

Trish Birtill

PLANET POEM

Darkness falls the stars come out,
The man in the moon puts his candles out,
Twinkling, sparkling, a shooting star,
Into the distance so, so far,
Is that a spaceship I've just seen,
Or airplane reflections in the gleam,
Is there life up in the sky,
Passing through us, flying by,
Are we being spied upon,
From Jupiter, Mars and beyond,
What a magical mystical place,
I'd like to investigate outer space.

Lucy Woodnutt

MY LITTLE LEMON TREE

I brought a little lemon tree, it looked so green and good,
So I put it in my sitting room, upon a shelf it stood,
My lemon tree was so beautiful and a picture of good health,
Until one day, a leaf fell off, I found it on the shelf.
I put it in another room as it struggled to survive
My lemon tree I watered to help it keep alive.
But one by one the leaves fell off, my lemon tree was dying,
I whispered gently 'Please don't die, don't ever give up trying.'
Then one day I noticcd a little shoot appear,
It seemed to say, 'Forgive me, I'll try again this year.'
The leaves began to grow again it filled me with delight,
My lemon tree did not give up, it put up such a fight.
My lemon tree is beautiful, its leaves are fresh and green,
It's back in all its glory, such a pleasure to be seen.
Oh how my little lemon tree depicted life for me,
While we accomplish all that's good, we blossom like the tree,
But when life's obstacles appear, we tend to fade and fall
We almost feel like giving up, it's not worth it after all,
But, as my little lemon tree, just rested for a while,
It then began to struggle back and its leaves began to smile,
So, if we sit back quietly, we will then in wisdom see,
Our characters are founded by setbacks just like these,
As God looks after little things like my small lemon tree,
I'm confident in His love and care, He looks after you and me,
So let's put our trust in Jesus, take Him to be our guide,
We can know and feel His presence, for
> *He's walking by our side.*

Joyce Berry

THE BEAR

In the attic room
There's an old teddy bear
Alone in the dark
In a small wooden chair

The light from the moon
Draws his shadow on the wall
The wind begins to whistle
As the rain starts to fall

Silent he is waiting
Sitting up straight
With a transfixed gaze
His pupils dilate

The room feels cold
On this August night
The bear looks ahead
Like he possesses sight

There's something about him
This strange little bear
Bought on impulse
From an antique fair

He appears to be happy
With his stitched on smile
But that's an illusion
Edwardian style

Kevin McSkelly

MOON BATHER

The Sun's unbroken, stainless bands
Girdling the Earth's high-curved walls,
Into night to the Moon's great platter
From where refracted, bent-light falls,
Through an open upstairs window
Falling in a planed figure of light
Standing in its bright-page cold-candescence.
On a night like this the garden's colour
Is more than a measure of its depth,
And looking from a window down
Is to reach into a harbour's warmth,
At the bottom purples, pebbles, mauves,
Cobalt-rock, herbaceous-reef ground-flower,
Anemone of sense silvery tendrils gripping earth,
Everything swims in the Moon's blue heat
And the great locked kelp of the trees
Hangs black in the high shallows,
As the yellow heads of daffodils
Bob uneasily like luminescent starfish
In a tropic night's lagoon,
Now a lunar surf breaks
Along the garden's edge,
Out of which come smiling muscled men
And women in starry bathing caps,
Swimming in the Moon's blue heat
Their gelatinous forms litter the garden air,
Undulating in and through the deepest blue,
I have been with them all the while
Moon-beams in the face and a cracked smile.

Stephen Hull

WEATHER MOODS

I just love watching rain
Running down my window pane
Rain falling from the sky
I think it comes from clouds that cry
The sun comes out to make them smile
And the rain stops after a while
A rainbow comes to join the fun
With the now happy clouds and sun
But the dark comes and spoils their play
So all three of them go away
The moon takes over followed by the stars
And then the planets including Mars
But you mustn't worry, the day will come
And then the clouds, the rainbow and the sun

Gemma L Daniel

REDUNDANCY

Thank you for your interest in us -
Please write clearly, stating first -
All my years of paper turning,
Inputting, prioritising (what a useful skill that is!)
What makes you feel you are able -
Why, the fact that people knew me,
Came to see me, asked me questions -
Said, what will they do without me?
What do you think you can offer -
Packed-up files of useless knowledge:
Names and corresponding numbers,
Recognising scrawls on jotters,
Knowing where to look for things.
Use this space to write your reasons -
They don't want me now. Do you?

Stephanie Dibden

WHERE IS PEACE?

Joyriders, muggers, drug-addicts who
        Spread their evil along the way
Are desperate beings but running from who?
        As they hide their deeds from the light of day
The old and infirm are their targets now
        No guaranteed safety can be hoped for
Just an everyday fight in an out and out war
        Why do they live this life that is useless?
A life without loving and caring is fruitless
        Can they not see the hurt that they cause
Forcing the old folk to stay behind doors?
        Doors that once stood open to all
To neighbours and any that cared to call
        But open house is a thing of the past
And walking the street in the light of day
        For many this is over, it is but a task
What is this greed that has got a hold
        On the youth of today? Makes the blood run cold
Never satisfied with what they have got
        No laughter, no joy in their lives do we see
But misery and heartache is their little lot
        Whilst parents and teachers fight for survival
Hope is eternal, prayers for revival of enriching lives
        Before they are lost
How long to get there and at who's cost?
        The youth of today must stop in their tracks
Before it's too late there's no going back
        No stroll in the park where once we felt safe
Leave the aged in peace, is it too much to ask?

Carole Hanson

WHERE HAVE ALL THE SLAG HEAPS GONE?

As I drive through valley and over bryn,
I see not things as they have been.

The dark grey hills are sorely missed
As I drive towards the distant mist.

Where once you smelled the acrid matter,
Are now diesel, pine and light industrial chatter.

The faces grey of those from down under,
Contrasted with those of the bath house wonder.

But now the red blown faces are all a-tanned,
From holidays had in a distant land.

As I move ever westward still,
I long to see those dark grey hills.

Oh, where have all the slag heaps gone?

O P Sed

UNTITLED

Six days a week, round about four,
A little girl comes to our door.
She's very welcome, on the dot,
She brings our Echo, does not stop.

All the news we want to hear
Adverts, pictures, they all appear.
A pleasant way to spend an hour.
Settle down, forget the shower.

Christmas time, just missed one day,
To all the staff, I'd like to say,
Thank you all, it's quite a pleasure
Our daily Echo, such a treasure.

J R Whitlock

SNOWDONIA

Misty mountains - sometimes snow-capped,
Often playing hide-and-seek.
Rolling hills all strewn with heather,
Softness underneath your feet.
Rowan trees ablaze with berries,
Busy little streams abound.
Walking somewhere - going nowhere,
Just be glad to be around.
Walking up beside the quarries,
Slate's the treasure that they gave,
Cottages now all in ruins,
Miners in an early grave.
Dark lagoons 'neath shady treetops,
Swans that live there gliding by.
Peace and beauty all around you,
Flowers, hills, and mountains high.
Wandering along the lakeside,
Still so peaceful - not alone.
Creatures that reside there - hiding,
Watching till you go back home.
If you're lucky p'raps a squirrel
Runs across your path ahead,
Darkness falls and owls are hunting
Tiny creatures out of bed.
Lovely just to wander round there,
Following on nature's trails.
Just can't wait to travel back
To a village tucked away in Wales.

Muriel Whitfield

UNTITLED

Empty glass, what a waste.
Don't commit a sin, put
it in the recycling bin.
Tonnes, and tonnes a day,
is rubbish that needn't be
thrown away.
With paper, and tins fill up
your recycling bins.
Renewable resources, are
but a few if you don't have,
the recycling view.
Global warming, heed the
warning. Let's make haste,
recycle waste, put it in
the proper place, and save,
the future generation race.

Averil Bond

TO BE ME!

To live!
To thrive!
To love!
To dance!
To smoke!
To breathe!
To create!
To break!
To grow!
To die!
To chain!
To be free!
To do what I want!
To be me!

Paul Lynch

WINTER IS HERE

The leaves are turning brown and falling,
The winter frost is calling,
And everybody's saying,
Winter is here.
Bonfires are alight,
And children won't sleep,
On the night that Santa Claus comes.

Rhiannon Smith (9)

IDLE THOUGHTS ON AN ITALIAN HOLIDAY

Oh foolish, frantic men of Rome
To follow Caesar far from home.
How could you find the time to tread
'long Hadrian's Wall and mine our lead?
Your legions must have loved our land
Of Celtic tribesmen - all half canned
On beer and painted all in woad
Meandering up your Roman road.
Our mud huts must have made you pine
For Tuscan villas and sunshine.
We've seen for what they must have yearned
And from the Britons what they learned.
Boodicca's chauffeur was no fool,
He opened up a driving school
For charioteers - those men of might
He taught to drive along the right.
'Gesticulate, maintain high speed,
Take corners wide, stay in the lead
And don't give way at all' he said.
My! How the Brits piled up the dead.
We know his pedagogic skill
Affects Italians even still!

Jim Bolter

IT DOESN'T MATTER

It doesn't matter where you come from
It doesn't matter where you've been.
It doesn't matter who you've met,
It doesn't matter what you've seen.
Along life's winding highway
With all its ups and downs.
It doesn't matter if you are famous
And lived life to the full,
Or merely scratched the surface,
And been considered rather dull,
You've had your share of happiness
And of sadness too!
You've tasted love and friendships
So life's been good to you.
It doesn't matter where you come from
Or if you've lived your dream,
It doesn't matter who you've met
It doesn't matter what you've seen.
What matters most of all,
When you reach that final bend,
All your troubles are behind you
When you reach the very end.

G Hatton

DAWN CHORUS

The blackbird yawned with gaping beak,
The crow just gave his mate a tweak,
The thrush in haste, swallowed some dew,
No noise came forth he just went blue.
Two jays not looking where they trod
Fell heavily on dampened sod.
Old sparrows in the eaves just stirred
But never chirped a blinking word.

And so all birds from slumber paused
Shook feathers, groaned, and stamped their claws.
Fear nought, the cold, or frost, or rain
The great deception starts again
For God has said that birds must sing
Each morning in the early spring.
Sore throats, bald rumps, none are excused,
Just so that humans are amused.

Denis M Pentlow

THE LIGHTHOUSE WATCH

Looking out from the far distant shore
Watching the sun set out at sea,
Dreaming of home so far away
Think of my love who waits for me.

Slowly as the night comes upon me
As the tide washes pebbles up the beach,
My friends, my family, and my sweet love
So far away, out of reach.

The moon arises and shines down from above
A solitary chime from afar doth ring,
My thoughts, entangled, but not for long
I ponder what the new day will bring.

Dawn comes my lonely vigil ends
I retire to bed and so to sleep,
To awake, arise and start again
My lonely watch out to sea I keep.

Colin Frederick Stewart

THE OTHER ISLAND

This Celtic land, this ancient place,
Has stared destruction in the face.
Mindless zealots with God on their side,
Attitudes people no longer abide.

A Northern majority swearing their loyalty,
Monopolies on God, Country and Royalty.
July parades, with sashes glorious,
Pledging allegiance in anthems victorious.

Nationalists saw a force of occupation,
Lost houses, jobs and segregation.
But with strength from the culture, they called their own,
They swore never to be bowed by an English throne.

So let those pure of heart and pure of deed,
Banish the paramilitary monster of greed.
It grew fat on the misfortune of others,
Fathers, brothers, sisters, mothers.
Lay it to rest for the next generation,
That we may live in hope and co-operation.

So pray your God gives guiding hand,
To help us heal this broken land.
Let bigoted souls of all persuasion,
Open their eyes to the illumination,
You cannot kill for peace . . .

Heather Steele

COLOURLESS AND GOLDEN

The beauty of love is in seeing others cry
is written on a wall of a room in a place
somewhere on another continent

The beauty of love is in crying out for space
is the mantra of inner-city life

Every morning, the sun-rises peach like the sun sets
Surrounding, in the balmy warmth
Touching in the heat of the moment the swallow
That flies from the shadow of the throat
To the scream of electric freedom wheeling in the skies
And the thunder rolls in, the heat breaks
Afternoon rain splashes our window.

Paul F Wort

MUCHLOVED

The town of Muchloved is no-man's town.
It lies robust within forgotten dreams
over sandstone lost to past seas.
Split asunder, it left holes in shadows,
memories of salt-water dried in crevices,
running free over old crock pipes.
Children played on slag heaps
thrusting darkness onto wondergreen
overlying all.
Cloth-capped workmen, my smithy-father, too,
walked to work on dusty roads
feet firm in horse-tracks.
We in Muchloved have lost all this -
we have progressed
and now live on concrete, pure and white.

Len Webster

SUITCASE

I've packed and re-packed it, My suitcase won't close.
Why I've packed all these shorts, I think nobody knows.
The winter is near. The summer is over,
I need a blue coat to go with my pullover.
Inside my small case I have everything together.
There's a sunhat, a raincoat and gloves for bad weather.
If I sit on it heavily, move my feet from the floor,
The suitcase might close, I'll be out the front door.
I need to close it before my train leaves,
So I hurry to tuck in the trousers and sleeves,
With one mighty leap and a sturdy right hip,
I close it at last, nearly breaking the zip.
I put on my trainers and head for the train,
I forget my umbrella so it's bound to rain.
By the time I am there I am tired and wet,
I jump with a startle, oh how could I forget?
I've not bought a ticket with all this great fuss,
So I'll have to be late by taking the bus.
Next time I won't take that last sock or my knickers,
My suitcase would shut and I might get there quicker.

Louise Salter

THERE'S MORE TO LIFE

There's more to life than meets the eye
The world just seems to pass you by
You're looking out on stony ground
but no-one seems to be around.

Inspiration seems to fail
Your mind is strangely rather pale
Life does not compute as such
and you can neither see nor touch
You try to touch but you don't feel
Nothing anymore is real.

It may not seem that clear to you
Just what it is you have to do
Open up your inner being
There's more to looking than just seeing
Lift your spirit to the sky
and only then you'll realise why

There's more to life than meets the eye

J Noice

THE LOVERS

They walked together on the shore
Two lovers hand in hand
They had each other, nothing more
But thought they owned the land

He saw the world within her eyes
His word was her command
Her rosy blush matched her bouquet
When she wore his wedding band

The years flew by and left their mark
Like water upon sand
His voice grown weak, her eyes now dim
Survey their world so bland

He looks into those faded eyes
And sighs at nature's plan
At time which creeps soft and unknown
To change the face of man

He bends to take her hand in his
To touch the golden band
Then she smiles and in her eyes
He sees two lovers hand in hand

Beryl Laithwaite

EIGHT MONTHS

Eight months pregnant, our first child
She's within the bursting bubble
The threatening savage on a thirsty scree
The river on its sure course
The waterfall.

Eight months pregnant, she's still mild
I'm without the cycle schedule
That threatening savage 'midst these coping cogs
The river from its pure source
To fatherhood.

I watch the stars, I read the plays
I sound confident to our neighbours
Do I?
I nurse the cries, I take the stage
I give Sunday School all my favours
And try . . .

She's faint, and I'm the rising dawn
She breathes at night, and I'm clock
Watching.
She's hot, and I'm the crystal lawn
She feels the swell, and I'm the boat
Holding.

Brett Milner

DÉJÀ VU

Let's get away,
By car, bi-plane,
By Train,
Who knows where it will lead,
To Anglesey or
Miami

Do you like coconuts?

Or maybe to Barking,
Where we can go larking (or mad!)

Or perhaps up to Troon,
Where you could make me swoon!
(Although you do that anyway)

Or let's go to Nantucket?
Maybe . . .?

Adrian P Shaw

MOTHERLESS LOVE

Her mother died
When she was young
She never knew
Her gentle kiss or hand
Was loved by sisters and aunts,
Grandmother in a darkened room,
In the sunshine she would play,
A smile was never far away,
Teaching stones with a teacher's
Stick
She would have order on the ground,
While her dreams were healing the sick.

She painted rainbow colours
With an artistic brush
Drew circles with her pen
Of her babies in a row
And when they came
Screaming, laughing or burping
She never said
I never had a mother of my own.

Patrick Cooper Duffy

MIND ALONE

Falling leaf, golden, twisting,
Shape and weight against wind resistance,
What force? Which angle? Can we find
The distance? Not felt by sky or surface
Waiting, mind alone, is aware
Of it's destination.

The wind in trees cause vibrations,
Changed to sounds when minds to please,
Gentle messenger, swiftly travelling
From trees to mind,
For recognition there to find.

Chemical reaction the flowers treasure,
Translated by mind to perfumed pleasure,
Scent of roses drifting in the breeze,
Like a miracle, puts mind at ease.

Magic within the food we need, from
Taste buds to mind, where divided
Sweet or sour, from the code
Locked up inside the seed.

Nerve ends, sensitive, ready waiting,
Sends signal to mind, of a gentle touch,
A message, from lips so tender,
Happy the mind, in love with the sender.

Terry Newman

MIDNIGHT MUSINGS

As I lay in my bed last night
(I couldn't sleep, try as I might)
Into my head there came a thought,
Unwanted quite, and quite unsought;

That every man and bird and beast
Is only such until deceased,
When their component parts diverse,
Their bonding broken, all disperse.

Through earth and water, worm and grass
Ex-bird, ex-beast, ex-man must pass,
Obeying all a common rule
They join the universal pool,
Whence recombining when they can
Become new beast, new bird, new man.

And then I thought I saw on high,
God watching this with loving Eye,
As combinations form and change,
Each one familiar, each one strange.

I fancy pleasure lights those Eyes
When luck assembles someone wise,
Or beauty's formed in limb or mind,
Or someone bothers to be kind.
I'd like to think that darkened looks
Would greet success for vicious crooks.

But wait!
I've gone too far, I'm being smart,
I have left out the soul and heart.
What do I know, I'm not God,
Only a temporary little bod!

Robert E Edwards

THE BRADFORD AND BINGLEY

I'm the man from the Bradford and Bingley
In the ads I wear a black bowler hat
I'm Mr Bradford I won't undersell you knowingly
Mr Bingley? He's in charge of the cash

I'm the voice of the TSB
I say 'Yes', to positive equity
We'll take your money invest it well
On a rainy day you can buy, not sell

But in real life, I get up at midday
After reading my mags and having a play
Watch Neighbours, ring my agent see what's in
If nought go back to bed with a big pink gin

I read the news on Radio 4
Pronouncing words like I'm at Primary School
Sound concerned with the news at the start
Give a little chuckle at the comical part

I got a job as a robber today
I withdrew from a Building Society
The Bradford and Bingley a tax-free lump sum
I read the news and told 'em what I'd done

I said give me the cash, to the bank that likes to say 'Yes'
Or I'll splat your brains, you'll look like Dali's best
Invest in me now, I'll spend it wisely
In the South of France at St Tropez
Disneyland in the US of A
On a sunbed in the Rose and Crown

Remember investments can go down as well as up
Remember too much Vodka and you're gonna throw up
Remember, remember before you forget
We don't really need you, we don't give a rip
You can die in the street boy, and we won't lose a cent

Gary Burt

A STROLL THROUGH URBAN ANARCHY

Well the night-club is rocking to Wagner
Backstage Siegfried he takes a little coke
Odin is drinking warm bottled larger
With a hammer Alberich's cracking jokes

Outside the sunset it has been stolen
It will be resprayed before it's resold
Behind the clouds whose dust will be falling
On pavements made of plastic and fools'-gold

People wander up into the jungle
With its hard light and its own techno sound
Where lives the bag lady with her bundle
Making her bed for the night on the ground

After half-past just before quarter-to
A church clock stutters its chimes through the night
Genghis the angel dressed in jeans of blue
On his Harley roars away to the fight

The cops hang around in their dressing-gowns
Ready and waiting to put you to bed
The china-doll has found a brand new clown
The burger man is wanting to be fed

A street corner looses its sharp angle
As cowboys and queens embroider its edge
Standing under an electric candle
Jesse James to Guinevere swears a pledge

Brother carry me over and under
Carry me over and under and through
From where the starling's song sounds like thunder
And hunger stands behind greed in the queue

Stephen Jackson

111

LIFE IN WINTER

Cold is the air in winter
      When all feel the pincher
Of the days of frost and snow
      Which makes your skins all aglow.

Rain beats down in a blowing cloud
      With a wind that blows so loud
Of guster sending trees and flowers
      Bowing down to the earth's deep bowers.

Sun warms the chill
      As you stroll up a hill
And wonder about life
      As like the weather.

P L Smith

THE LOST SLEEPER

Late, past bedtime, past the last light.
      The wind bellows against the pane
shakes the house and rattles the glass.
      Rain and gale rule the world:
a Storm King rumbling and grinding.
      How frightened am I, a little mouse
in the spacey, empty box that is my room.

      As far as any could see, I am all alone
with no yielding arms to give me warmth,
      a continent-spanning bed to lie in,
and hours to blow by before the dawning.
      Yet you are there with me, a golden dream
whose love and gentleness leaves traces longer
      than the imprint of your head and body
on the sheets and pillows could ever last.

Adam Manning

RESPECTABILITY

The old woman sat, smugly smoothing down her skirt
To cover her arthritic knees. (She would not flirt
With druggies, drunks or drop-outs - Society's dregs -
By allowing them a glimpse of her gnarled, old legs!)

Then she scattered crumbs to feed the pigeons; plump birds
That milled around her as she whispered gentle words
Of endearment. Charity's not out of place
For them it seems - just for the human race.

Pauline Mackey

A STRANGER IN A STRANGE LAND

I was a stranger in a strange land,
In *Strangeways* 1962.
A strange man,
In a strange way,
Told when to eat and what to do.

Strange ways weren't my ways,
In *Strangeways 1972.*
Those were strange days,
In *Strangeways,*
They had strange sexual habits too.

I was an old man,
In an old land,
In *Oldham* 1982.
My hair was greyed and teeth decayed,
My glasses held with glue.

I was a lonely man in a free land,
Released in British 1992.
I think it requisite
To pay them a visit,
In *Parkhurst* 2002.

Rick Ford

THOSE PRECIOUS DAYS

There are no words that I can say,
To ease the parting ways,
When friendship such as ours is tossed,
Forever lost, those golden days,
Upon the sea of time, within the haze
Of sombre hours, my grief resides,
Where sorrow walks too deep for tears,
And loneliness abides.
The echo of your laughter rings,
When time has conquered pain of
Hard remembrances, the songbird sings
And I have learnt in lighter hours
To live again, forgive me, if my thoughts
Stray, now and then to you on gilded wings.

Susan Erskine

THE BOOKCASE

I must tidy up the bookcase sometime
The Argos catalogue lies across
The Ascent of Everest which I bought in a jumble sale
and I thing has got mildew
like The School in the Forest written by Angela Brazil
that belonged to my mum.
Then there's a lottery ticket in Scott Fitzgerald
and Women in Love is next to The Prince.

I don't know why a toy dustcart
is parked on top of The Concise Oxford English Dictionary
I know I don't want to open The Pooh Birthday Book
to see whose birthdays I've forgotten.
People are coming round Thursday night
you should see the rest of the room
then again maybe you shouldn't.

Jane Brady

LOVE IS

Love is the strongest thing on earth,
Apart from grief and pain.
I'm sure that I will never know,
The like of it again.

Love is that feeling deep in your heart,
That will never fade away.
It happens very quickly,
And in your heart will stay.

Love can be good love can be bad,
Love is a thing of great joy.
Love can come when you least expect it,
To any girl or boy.

Love can make you happy,
And love can make you sad.
Love can make you miserable,
And love can make you glad.

Love can make your heart feel light,
Or a burden of your life.
If you find the one you love is gone,
It can cause you grief and strife.

True love comes from one alone,
And it can rule your life.
And you find that special person,
Just once in your life.

So if you feel you love someone,
Don't wait too long when you're sure.
Or you'll hate yourself forever,
Believe me there is no cure.

John Lugg

TEARS ON THE WINDOW PANE

Like tears on the window pane
To wash away the memory,
Falling, falling, cold clear rain,
Consigning our love to history.

You fled in the fading light
To start a new life far away,
Running, running, through the night,
With nothing here to make you stay.

Sad songs filled with heavy rhymes
Thud hard around my aching head,
Ticking, tocking, the clock chimes,
Time drags on with a heart of lead.

I recall lost summer days
Spent sitting by the trickling stream,
Lazy, lazy, in the haze,
Now, alas, it is just a dream.

This love for you I could not hide
Beneath the darkest, thickest cloak,
Yearning, yearning, deep inside,
Fiery passion burns through the smoke.

Come in from the raging storm,
Into my arms where you belong,
Cosy, cosy, in the warm,
Then you will see our love grow strong.

Robert J Lambert

LOVE'S VICTORY SONG

When! cried I, shall the nightingale arise
And kill the hawk who hunts the skies,
When shall the raven be slain by a dove
That death would fall to boundless love;
Why O Lord, can't I, like Thee,
Arise from my cross to victory,
And learn the law of love in rhyme
You make all things beautiful in your time.

Conquering love, and patient virtue, Lord show me the way,
When they took you in the garden
Peter's sword of wrath you stayed,
Within cruel pilot's mocking hall - spoke not a vengeful word
So they marvelled at your dignity
Yet crowned with thorns, my God,
O! show me gentle Saviour - this strength of love impart
Just give one beat - one drop of blood
From that blessed, sacred heart.

Teach me your acceptance of a heavenly Father's will,
That stayed your angels' righteous wrath
Around Golgotha's Hill,
And bore the sins of men who'd pierced you
Whom you did no wrong,
Crying 'Father please forgive them' 'Twas your enemy's love song;
My Lord you knew what they could not
Still they mocked your cries to Heaven,
Yet the angel sang to Magdelene, the nightingale prince has risen.
To you Hell's power, of sin and death, o'er man, its realm
relinquished.
O! Nightingale dove, your infinite love, has all evil's might now
vanquished.

T A Elliott

EVACUATED CITY

City, say farewell to your children,
this quiet army marching from your arms.
Watch them and stand brave.
For they take with them your colour,
leaving grey and dull your veins
and cold your cobbled pores.
They take with them your passion,
leaving stillness but not peace,
across your stone clad frame.
They take with them your music,
leaving discord in your voice
and flat your dulcet tones.

City, say farewell to your children,
this army bumping gas masks on their knees.
Watch them and stand brave.
For they do not take your glory,
or the valour from your heart
- the daring of your nerve.
And they do not take your courage
or the boldness of your spirit
- the virtue of your dreams.
As you distract their danger
and harbour all their pain,
remember they are safe.
Watch them and stand proud.

Angela Rogerson

FLOTSAM AND JETSAM

The river lazily flows by,
as I lie stretched out on my mossy bed.
Idle thoughts wither and die,
as the suns reflection skims on the oily river.
This river has its rhythms like any other,
and I let its blues fill my head.
The reverie ended - I enter the metropolis.
The human tide washes through the streets,
the sound of many feet move to the beat of the clock.
A piece of discarded flotsam sits at the side of the street,
gazing unseeing at the endless stream before him.
A man in blue moves on, *cause begging's not allowed here.*
Back then to the polish and the tinsel now flotsam has been removed
But where's Jetsam?
Here comes Jetsam - he's left the tavern.
A thousand curses resound invisible around his red face
as he enters the throng.
Even the trees don't look real here,
pruned and sheared,
their arms cannot reach to the sun.
They all look sad, they all look blue.
The small ornamentals remind me of fluffy poodle dogs,
very distant relations to the ones at the river.
So back there I go,
where the trees grin with the wryness of centuries of knowledge,
and nature watches you
walking through its domain.

Tristan Brown

ODE TO A MAIDEN

O! Fair maiden of eighteen summers pass'd,
Thy beauty nourish'd by creams and secrets
And thy looking-glass,
Prithee harken to my song:

Lo! Thy glass is ev'ry windowpane
In ev'ry tavern wherein oft we'd recline,
Thy sweet ears hearing ev'ry conversation
But mine.
Thine eyes, lustrous orbs of sham,
Divining ought
But mine.

So passeth we many an eve
Whilst I (a devious varlet) would ply thee
With roguish sack,
To later aid my base desires,
Chamberwise.

Zounds, but thy lips were soft
And forsooth marble-smooth thy thighs,
But I wonder by my troth
Why a fair maid like thee
(so randy and oozing with vitality)
Wouldst thou only make love . . .

With your clothes on.

Brendan McCusker

HUNGRY

The world would be a better place
If people learnt to share
There could be a lot more peace in the world
As everyone would care.

There is so much selfishness about
While millions die of starvation
There's not much hope for these poor souls
Deaths rise up in devastation.

Young children and mothers with babes in arms
Lie waiting their turn to die
There's so much we take for granted
Just watch the TV, it will make you cry

We waste food every day of the week
Factories dump loads each day
While the millions suffer quietly
All they can do is pray

Factories dump items because they are broken
With food its just the box
So while the contents are dumped in the yard
The factories tied up like Fort Knox

Pop along to your local factory
Where they've dumped maybe sweets galore
They won't even let you buy them
So the crime rate is a lot more

Why should we be allowed to waste so much
With what you see on the telly
While millions would be in their glory
With one grain of rice in their belly.

Maggie Hutt

WHALES

Cruising along in the sea,
with hardly any effort,
are to be seen some large and beautiful creatures.
Who, just for their meat and other substances,
are yearly killed, or maimed by harpoons.

These beautiful creatures
are kings and queens of many oceans,
and majestically they swim in many seas.
With their large tails to steer themselves with,
they move along in the open sea.

These mammals who do man no harm
yet, are killed mercilessly by man
for his own purposes.
But still I wonder why this should be,
for these vessels should not be used for food.

These mammals,
who are the true denizens of the deep,
have their beauty in their graceful movement.
And, if each and every one were killed,
the seas and oceans would be a silent world.

A T Saunders (15)

AFTER YOU'VE GONE

The future was always beckoning
When we would have to part.
How could I acknowledge the reckoning
Would be the breaking of my heart.

Love true, deep and without measure
My future was always your choice
Heartfelt memories always to treasure
The emptiness no longer filled by your voice.

The bluebells will grow and bloom
And you and I will survive
The shadows creep across the room
And what's the point in being alive

We grabbed the chance to live these years.
The reckoning seemed so far away -
But here I sit alone in tears
The bill has to be paid today.

Mary Williams

A DEATH IN SPRINGTIME

Brass, wood, light and shadow,
Amethyst and bronze.
The lilies' limpid sensuality is poised.
Tomorrow their decline.
Still hidden beneath the firmness of their petals,
Decay envelopes their innermost cavities.

Tomorrow their gift will have been given,
Their offerings presented.
Like she who was the helmet maker's beautiful wife,
They will become downcast, cast off, cast out.

Their place before the cast iron fire,
Cold at spring's onset,
Remembers its heat at winter's height,
Glowing in January.
Fire on ice.

Amen. Requiescant in Pace.
Deo Gratias.

Michael Lyons

NEVER TRUST MEN WITH TATTOOS

Do not trust men with tattoos
A piece of advice
my mother never gave me.
Never trust men with tattoos
Unless it be a most modest one
of a small butterfly or bird
winging,
Perhaps on the outer place
of the neck
or the inside
of the thigh.
My lover wore eye make-up sometimes
as dark as bruises.
Those glances
are left behind
on my heart
But
never trust men with tattoos
a piece of advice
my mother never gave me.

Stevie James

I WILL REMEMBER YOU

When I walk through waves
      On cold wet sands
And see the suns golden hue.
      Watch lovers walking hand in hand
Then I will remember you

On dark still nights
      When the moon is gold
And the sky is the darkest blue
      In the peace and stillness of that night
I will remember you

When I hear guitars playing
      And certain words they are singing
When I hear songs old and new
      As I hear each song and feel each note
I will remember you

Alexandra Garrard

THE BREACH

A gun-shot splits the air
Resounding, whip-like
Across the back of morning.
Milling rocks erupt in flight
Spilling down from tall thin trees.
Assurance has been tangled with
Now rabbits quiver in their darkness
Praying, frantic to evade
The hands that shatter peace.

Those nameless hands
That claim the day
That rob the complex
Of its store.
Those heartless eyes
That aimed out life
Those blackened eyes
That flamed the roar.
What vow knows iron
Twinned with flesh?
What conscience has this beast?
Skilled in deprivation are
The hands that shatter peace.

A W Bullen

DISCONTENTMENT

How it rages within me
Like a vicious, angry storm
How can this be
So strong, so deep?
Like a huge well
Large beyond measure
Robbing me of life's pleasures
What is the cause?
What is the root?
What is the cure?
Let me pause and meditate
How to purge this soot
From my soul
The deep depths within me
So that all may see
A happier, contented me
Truly, truly desire to be.

Sharon McLafferty

THE BREAKING OF THE BREAD

God made the wheat to give us bread.
God made the grape to give us wine.
God took them in His Hands, and said,
     'Eat - drink,
      This is My Life Divine.'

The wheat is ground to make it bread.
The grape is crush'd to make it wine.
'God, take me in Thy Hands,' I said,
     'Grind - crush
      My life, and make it Thine.'

Dominic R Whitnall

DROWNING

Look.
Sea; the two of us
controlled by a lunar influence.
       I am a woman.
You are two; when we join
and dive below
then surface, gasping for breath:
       Overwhelmed
       I am you.
       And you listen
to your words
that trickle from my lips
then rise like bubbles
to enter another world.
       And yet, down here they remain:
       Unheard
       Save by our own souls.

JLP

TREASURES

My treasures are not jewels rare,
Or heavy chests of gold.
But in the bright and lovely things
That cannot be bought or sold

A child's soft hand clutched tight in mine,
A good friend tried and true,
A sunset in a burst of flame
And stars in misty blue.

A garden filled with flowers fair,
And birds upon the wing,
My treasures lie in loveliness,
Then I have everything.

David Blair

TIME TO MOVE ON

Everyone's running away, just like me
It will be good to see them being free
But my bleeding heart cries for me to stay
Because all it does is drip, every day

The hanger-on's no longer call
So I won't have to build that wall
But demons still run around my room
And my ex' still flies on her broom.

I stopped going to the Prison every day
They promised I will be back to stay
My love is stripping at my door
So we won't waste any time before hitting the floor

The pub on the corner is going to close
It will soon re-open called *The Wilting Rose*
Someone must have broken the landlord's heart
Because it used to be called the *Golden Tart*

Everyone has been telling lies
That they are happy and will never die
Just like people who dig graves
They will have to be brave

I think I will move on in disgrace
I'm tired at having to plead my case
I'm innocent but always getting sent down
And the Judge does it with a smile, never a frown

Andrew Curtis

HONOURED LADY OF OUR LAND

Epitome of graciousness through many, many years,
First Lady of our nation in times of toil and tears,
We greet you as your birthday comes with memories sublime;
You're numbered with the century, as keeping step with time.

From Scotland's hills you won the heart of him who would be king;
As wife of our King George the Sixth, joint thankfulness we bring.
Through years of war and days of stress almost beyond belief
Your quiet presence in the storm spoke of respite and relief.

Enduring with your people then through days of dark distress
Ensured your place within the hearts of all who would address
Their minds to thoughts of righteousness and peace, and contemplate
The heritage and history that have made our nation great.

In God's good time, as we recall, was tyranny destroyed
And once again could England be in gainful tasks employed.
In such short time you moved aside, eternity had called
And through long years your dedication has us all enthralled

As to your varied duties you still wide attention give.
Vitality and friendliness we see each day you live,
Personifying *grandma* to the families of our land
Who still retain old concepts that by God Himself were planned.

They all today would welcome you if you could pay a call
Grand Lady of our heritage, admired by one and all
They'd welcome you, I know they would, with open, out-stretched arms
And greet you as befits a Queen, Elizabeth of Glamis

R J Carnell

DO NOT DISTURB

If they come out to ask us why
We photograph their door, their steps.
The windows from the side,
And learning our reason then invite us in
Should we be tempted, now, to step inside?

Might there be radiators where
The bevel-mirrored, handsome hearths
Diametered the family circle, close-grouped and whole
With placing of settee and chair and little stool,
Towards the radiant coal.

Ascending stairs perhaps we'd pause halfway
Admire some ornament or flower display,
Mourning the battered, old, tin toffee box
From which each riser quickly chose
A crisp, fresh handkerchief for each long day.

The back room cannot be the same, we see
The side extension, very neatly done;
But banished the angled window trimly cornering
The table with its brown chenille which caught
The sunshine, golden as we came to tea.

Better to stay in safe, long-distance shot,
Noting the features which remain secure,
The verge, the too-grown trees, the little wall,
The stained-glass tuliped entrance to the narrow hall, and hold
Secret and safe the occupation as it was before.

Mollie B Moor

A SONNET TO VANESSA REDGRAVE

She is a thespian, born of a thespian line,
Whose regal presence dominates the stage.
Her classic features, hardly touched by age,
Were finely sculpted to a grand design.

Using her skill and talent, she portrays
A Scottish teacher or Egyptian queen,
Bringing a special magic to each scene
Wherein her craft will dazzle and amaze.

Her dulcet tones, with muted resonance,
Charm and bewitch our sensibilities,
Creating for us an ephemeral trance
Which soothes the spirit, and can coax and tease
Our willing minds to join the great romance
Which she dispenses with artistic ease.

Celia G Thomas

GYPSIES

Gypsies in my garden
Washing line a'bobbing.
There they are hobnobbing
Iridescent feathers gleam,
Reflect winter's feeble gleam
Just like a country market,
Gossip chatter noise and natter.
Frizzled fat, breadcrumbs and suet,
I really marvel where they put it,
Pecking order counts for nowt,
First one in is last one out.
Oh! Dear me! Here comes that cat,
Rush of wings they rise and soar,
Back tomorrow they'll be for more
Starlings! My gypsies of the air.

H G Loveless

ANOTHER TIME, ANOTHER PLACE

What feeling is this
That invades my thought?
My judgement it clouds
My conscience it distorts.

Just under the surface -
Something I can't explain
Not to be seen or touched
But its memories remain.

No promise has been broken
And nothing has been said,
But discomfort holds my hand
And guilt is in my head.

A distant background tingle
I am constantly aware
Trying to ignore it
But knowing it is there.

Useless moments of pleasure
A knowing little smile,
Just flirting with my ego
And believing it for a while.

Siobhan Lees

KILLING REGRET

Why is it that on the brightest day
the hounds of hell can spring in my way
with all my mistakes of the past?
They torment me until, at last,
survival instinct rescues me.
Switch on the radio, hear a voice.
Don't care what, I have no choice.
Anything to stop the pain I feel
when thoughts make it all so real
again - curse my memory.
They can't make a drug that kills regret.
I know that you have forgiven me, and yet
until I can forgive myself, and leave
the past where it lies and cease to grieve;
I know there is no hope for me.

Gillian Avis

BROKEN

Eyes cry - but hearts bleed,
The body aches and has great need
Of you, your smile, your love,
But you flew away like a frightened dove.

Hard words I wrote, but true,
Because it seemed you knew not what to do?
You need not have been so hard and cruel
For I wanted nothing, I was not a fool.

Your company was all I asked.
Now you're gone and the past is masked
With broken hearts and broken smiles.
Your now far, far away one hundred miles.

Jane Webber

DEMENTIA

Life's patterns change through the years
Insidiously you developed this cruel disease
From a bride to a mother, a widow, a dear friend
A sister, a grandmother with grandchildren to attend
Now confusion increases and exhaustion never ceases
On endless walks you pace to and fro - no peace.
From a brain that gives you no rest
Bless you, yet you try to do your best
No respite from your restlessness
No time to stop and eat
Not even medication keeps you off your feet
Your face is strained and bewildered
A shadow of your former self
Yet in life you were patient, loving and kind
No faults in people did you find
We value who you are
As we love and give you care.

Ann C Younger

THE POOL

From my recumbent position in a striped deckchair,
I see a child making his way to the rocky mass,
Hidden by a huge peaked cap and shrouded in a tee-shirt,
To keep out the sun's harmful rays.
A tiny man-cub this one, stick thin brown limbs and wispy blond hair.
He stops, and chooses carefully from a pile of wet pebbles by the rocks.
The hand that plucks the stone is small, an infant warrior,
The thin brown arm raised back, plop, the joyous sound of a pebble in a pool.
Two tiny feet splash rhythmically at the water's edge.
Crouching down now, an easy position of the young.
Minute fingers dip and swirl in the waters salty warmth.
A perfect time for one small boy at one with the elements, by the seashore.

Patricia J Castle

MY GARDEN FUN

Out in the garden so full of space
I feel the warm summer sun on my face
I have a swing and a slide to climb
Mum plays with me so I feel safe all the time
My dog likes rushing all around
And sometimes he knocks me down on the ground
Still I know that he loves me, he's real ace
He helps me up and licks my face
See the asters, nicotiana, delphiniums, so tall
Antirrhinums and lilies I know and love them all
The roses are really the ones that I love
Their fragrance seems to come from Heaven above
Mum says God created all flowers big and small
He also made the bees to pollinate them all
Even the buttercups and daisies in the lawn
Must have had a reason to be born
Look how this pansy has found a spare space
You see I am blind and can't see its face
But don't think that I can't enjoy
Just like any other little girl or boy

My mum tells me what they are like
As I ride around the garden, on my bike
Don't pity me, feel sad, or cry
My fingers tell me as much as your eye
Now that I am learning, it's a wow
'Cos dad's put their names on, in Braille
You are attracted to the colours I can tell
I like the velvet softness and the smell
When I leave school to face the world full of hope
With my parents love to guide me I am sure I will cope

M J Streatfield

135

A RUGGED OLD STRANGER

I trudge the streets, from dawn to dusk,
With no-one to care and no-one to trust.
The world rushes by, too blind to see,
A rugged old stranger, who's living most free.

I'm not like the rest and have to have all.
I've got what I want, freedom to call.
To call to the Lord and ask from down here,
Where are you now, when I need you the most.

Sitting alone, resting my back on a post.
Your stars are my blanket, the earth my bed.
With me in the middle, a tear I sometimes shed.
I know I have nothing, but the clothes on my back.

So I ask you Lord, don't turn your back,
Please come to me and share my load,
As we walk together, along the road.
A friend I have found, to give me most cheer,
A friend and a partner, that is so very dear.

J Munday

ENDING

My mind was spiteful
And grey as the weather
So I took her umbrella

The year had seen
          moments of joy
But I could not see through
          The rain on my glasses

Quietly
She got wet.

Giles Whitehead

THE HONEY GIVERS

'Old Booth always busy at his bees
Found a cure for Isle of Wight disease'

My pupil gave me a gift of honey.
I gave it to the man who told me about 'Old Booth' -
A second grandfather to the man when he was a boy.

Now the man, father like to me, both of us childless,
Tells of his childhood, my father as child -
All about the village hive where our families
pre-electric lived and worked and had their being -
Living to survive and surviving to live amidst
the honeysuckle, heather, rambling rose and rasps.

Now, all gone - only the bees remain the same,
unelectrified, they work on,
Given life by Old Booth, they have, like me,
a function to fulfill -
But I, his great grandson,
See to honey of a different kind.

My life is a school, my queen, education
My honey is knowledge, my workers are pupils -
Their pollen is my work for them -
So honey must and does get given
The sweet lubricant of life and
Given and received in fullness in everything of the best.

D G Boothroyd

BEST FRIEND

I look in my mirror and what do I see?
I see my best friend looking back at me.

She is the one who helps me through
With whatever I say and whatever I do.

If I am feeling sad and near to tears
She reminds me of the happy carefree years.

If I have done something wrong or out of spite
She is the only one who can put things right

If I stop and chat to someone for a while
She is the one who can make them laugh and smile

If there is something I really, really want to do
She is the only one who can make it come true.

When I am feeling sorry for myself and don't know what to do.
She reminds me by saying 'There are a lot worse off than you.'

So pull yourself together tomorrow is another day
And just like magic my cares and woes seem to fade away.

You also have a best friend like me.
Just look in your mirror and you will see,

Yvonne Stephens

TO A ROSE

Oh lovely rose thou art so fair,
Thy beauty unsurpassed.
Thou art the sweetest flower that grows,
Thy petals pure and chaste . . .

I've watched thee grow from day to day,
Small bud to heavenly bloom.
Thy scent and fragrance fill the air,
And rid my world of gloom.

To me thou art the virgin's flower,
Thy stem a *crown of thorns*
When dewdrops form upon thy face,
Like for thy dear son mourns.

And very soon you'll fade and die,
When winds with *passions* roar.
But you will rise again next year,
More lovely than before.

Mary P Linney

ANOTHER GREAT SATURDAY

It begins pleasantly enough.
'Going for a couple of pints, love, before the rugby
Come if you like.'
'No thanks I'll finish tidying up.'

The first hint of trouble comes a few hours later.
'Just brought a few of the lads back. You don't mind
do you?'
Beer cans, ashtrays and muddy boots adorn the newly-cleaned carpet.
Regardless of weather, shopping seems a better alternative.

Spend time in the bookshop, the chemist - even the Co-op,
Knowing what awaits at home.
Arrive in time for the final whistle.
'Off to drown our sorrows - you missed a great game.
Back soon - I'll just have a couple of pints.'

Three hours later, eternal optimism has taken another knock.
Put the dinner in the microwave, or the dog,
And settle down to watch the Gladiators.

Another great Saturday!

Loraine A Aitken

THE ARMS DEALER

He rubs his hands and is content
Thinking his money's been well spent.
He's pleased to know he's bought his share
Of the arms at this year's fair.

But he never thinks ahead
Or sees the people lying dead.
He cannot hear the children's cries
Or see the bombs rain from the skies

He lifts his infant from his cot,
Thinking how fortunate his lot.
He knows he never will be poor
Because his future's quite secure.

the tragic plight of the refugee
Is something else he cannot see,.
In cold and wet they're forced to roam
Whilst he owns a splendid home.

His child did not obey his will,
Now his plans for him fulfil.
A soldier's what he chose to be
And later went across the sea.

A telegram then came which said
That his precious son was dead.
Adding to his grief and pain
He'd by a British bomb been slain.

Then the father went quite wild
Because he'd lost his only child.
He'd come to realise too late
The harm that's caused by tools of hate.

Margaret Harrison

BOSNIA ETC . . .

It's a place, how near I don't know but how
        far it must be:
For ignorance is rife, sentiment rare.
Fading in and out of our lives if it touches
        us at all,
We wait with that unseeing glare.
Another death, but what do we care?

Appearance is strangely familiar.
Brand names of cars and clothes,
May trigger some emotion.
Locked away in a *Desert Storm,*
What can we do?

Children who grew up lost in a world which
        once shared their dreams,
A world now celebrating a great success,
An invention, remembrance or two,
While current agony goes unseen:
When can their mourning begin?

Sleep in your beds tonight, do please,
Though wait a few years, for they will pass by,
When all that is cherished is a nation-wide lie,
How everything was done yet nothing help,
Those poor desperate people; their plight
        and their prayers.

Now ponder this question, was it right
        to dismiss,
The voice of the people, where no
        distinction is heard?
From their unanswered prayers,
        denied in silence.
Well, you might have made time,
But the problem, was theirs.

Sarah Louise Heathcote

A SMILE IN A CROWD

A Queen who passes for a Queen
We hold by perpetuity of her smile,
Not for diadems alone
Or all the sheaves of office do we concede to her,
Not by the stance of statehood bold
Or pre-emptive sanguinary issue,
Nor by the figurine of worship
Do we couch commendation of her soul
But by the hold sweet providence brings
To such minds charitably disposed to find it.

Anthony White

ONE-SIDED LOVE

They say 'one kisses and the other turns the cheek'
As our lives entwine
I pour the wine
And know
The cheek is thine.
And because thine the submissive cheek
Thine, too, the sword
And mine the bared breast
Exposed to the wound you choose to inflict
Where others might have caressed.
Deep is the hurt when after love
Your cold eyes conceal
The hint of love and tenderness
Which others would reveal.
They say that 'one accompanies and the other call the tune'
As our lives entwine
I pour the wine
And know
The song is mine.

Nona Mankelow

WINTER DEPRESSION

Sometimes I'd like to end this life
It's too much struggle, too much strife
I'd like to sleep and never wake
No more lonely tears or pain to take

When you're living on your own
You cannot call your house a home
A lot of friends will come and go
The way you feel, they'll never know

I cannot show the hurt inside
Sometimes I'd like to run and hide
Instead I'll face the world and smile
And keep on pushing, mile by mile

It's when I'm on my own at night
I have to fight this lonely fight
No-one to turn to and no-one to hold
Empty house and bed that's cold

No loving arms to comfort me
To share my hurt and really see
The feelings that are in my head
The times I wish that I was dead

But I've come so far, I can't let go
Just because I'm feeling low
I've worked too hard and done so well
To give up the fight for one bad spell

Cathie Hurcombe

143

LUCY'S ROOM!

Please clean your room Lucy,
Please try to set it straight,
Please clean it now Lucy,
It really cannot wait.

Lucy doesn't listen,
Lucy doesn't hear,
Besides, it can't need doing,
She did it just last year.

L Stuttard

MOVEMENT AT LAKE EYRE

No footmarks here disturb
      a low flat surface of the earth
Skeletons are all that tell
      preserved by salty dearth
The crunchy cracky feeling
      underneath moving feet
Feel they'll never find their way again
      into a civilised beat
Sky moves on unheeding
      the further that you walk
And the prize which you would capture
      of the shining shimmering salt
Moves on
and on
and on
Whilst sand dunes and samphire
      play their merry mirage game
Where everything is doubled
      then doubled yet again
Oh widest lake and sky
      may I visit when I die

Olive Knudsen

FEAR

Lord, I am scared:
Scared to love,
For to love will risk rejection.
I am scared of the strength
Of my imperfection.
Scared of the past.
Scared of today.
Scared of the hugs
I can never repay
I am scared of myself
And these feelings of pain
Scared to walk back
Down memory lane
I am scared of the person
I cannot be.
But even more scared
Of staying as me.

Joanna Grant

MEMORIES

I remember clearly the excitement of it all,
The lengthy days of waiting the feel of walking tall,
I'd never felt this way before, nor wished the months to fly,
But of a sudden, here I was with thoughts that made me cry

'Twas happiness that made me cry, I couldn't comprehend
The emotions that I felt, and will I ever understand
That waiting for a baby is a wonderful event
E'en though I feel this mixture of emotions truly spent

And now with every passing day, I live it all again
The days of pleasure, days of joy and even days of pain.
The daughter that I bore with pride so many years ago
Oh joy! Is giving birth herself and will rejoice I know.

Zena A Horton

SHARING A LABORATORY

Sharing a laboratory.
All rats in the same maze as we scurry for food.

But I like the twitch of your tail,
It pleases me above all others.

And I like the sound of your squeak,
It comforts me so.

And I like the wrinkle of your nose,
The way it sends your whiskers quivering
In a manner so like my own.

Sharing this laboratory -
With you.
It would be cold and lonely if you were not here.

Steph Hendry

MOVING

I gaze at packing cases full of books
with gloom, unable to decide or choose
between which ones are favourites or what looks
more useful - A to Z or *Ballet Shoes.*
A move from family house to match-box size
means clearing out one's mind, beset with fears
of losing precious memories besides
the LP disks and tatty souvenirs.
Why do we dream and agonise so much?
The loss of comfort, like a well-worn shoe,
is hard and leaving nearby friends is such
a wrench, none will be so reliable.
Detachment is a treasure that one finds,
like monk or nomad, frees us from what binds.

Margaret Wilson

146

ACROSS THE RIVER

That dark tunnel which lies ahead.
The one which some sincerely dread.
I fear no evil, for I see
The light of heaven beckons me
And on that day those angel wings.
Will come and gently carry me.
Across the river which divides.
And then my Saviour I shall see.

To kneel and kiss those feet so torn
To feel the nail prints in his hands
And he will lovingly gather me
Where on his bosom I shall lie.

The tears all gone no grieving heart
No more the tempter at my heels.
But blessed Saviour of my heart
Among the chosen I shall stand.

But now I must be quite content,
To do his will on earth
To cry the tears and weep
For all who know him not.

Oh God my prayer to thee is this
Help me show others what they miss
In me, Oh God let thy light shine
So they can know that I am thine

Millie Wallace

UNTITLED

There's a party up in Heaven, when a sinner's saved,
Because the name of Jesus, on their heart's engraved.
Given life abundant, freedom from the past,
Now in life eternal, this world we've now surpassed.

The angels up in Heaven, with instruments are playing,
Dancing to the music, their joyousness displaying.
The timbrels and the harps, the Heavenly choir is singing,
Praise God Hallelujah, voices now are ringing.

Joined with Heavenly host, we worship and we praise,
Protected by His blood, now promised all our days.
Shout our acclamation, Jesus Christ's alive,
Breathe Your breath upon us, Spirit now revive.

Take us Holy Spirit, into realms unknown,
Direct us Holy Spirit, and help us reach Your throne.
Let us feel Your presence, a touch from You we need,
Thank you Abba Father, we are privileged indeed.

Your blessing's now upon us, anointed by Your hand,
If we live a thousand years, we'll never understand
Just why we're chosen vessels, plucked from Satan's hold,
Now refine us with Your fire, to come forth as Your pure gold.

Ann Driver

THE BEDROOM

A tasteless, turquoise, T-shirt,
strung over a shiny stainless -
steel shower tap.

A modern motionless midi hi-fi
brings the dull, drab, dark
corners of the room to life.

'Booom, booom, booom', as a bouncy,
boisterous, beat stirs a subtle
silent stranger.

Covers clash with the curtains, cupboard
and the carpet, colourful framed
lines lacerate a laconic style.

Many times, many people,
have given *much respect*
to my Bedroom!

James T Oakley (14)

OUR LAND

I walked through fields of grasses uncut,
I passed an old man in his hut,
Through woods and lanes, I wandered alone,
In this place we call home.

Far in the distance I heard a scream,
Of an animal lost from sight,
But soon he would find what was his
Where a stream does flow through the night.

What caught my attention was something fine,
A bird singing way up in the pine,
A rabbit ran home to his borrow
As a hedgehog scrambled into the furrow.

The grasses were swaying in the breeze,
The soft low voices of the trees,
As they sang a lulling song,
But soon this had to end, as along came the rain,
Then it was all gone.

Anne Philippot-Prowse

A GAME OF TWO FACES

It's a game of two faces,
When you sing with two voices
And you can play this game better than I,
For one voice is sweet,
- It's the voice when we meet you,
But the other sings only with lies.

Now trust is a sure thing,
A good and a pure thing,
But it's damaged when you play this game,
So don't be unjust now
- And abuse people's trust now
'Cos to lose it would be such a shame.

This game of two faces
 - Plays on false circumstances,
and it deals out injustice and lies,
It cares not for our feelings
- With its bitter misdealings
Nor the casualties it brings to our lives.

It makes me feel wounded,
- Hurt and down-hearted,
Betrayed and back-talked and sore,
So take your game of two faces
And stick it up your places,
'Cos I wish to play it no more.

Paul Andrews

MOTORISTS' JARGON

Is a dipstick stupid or a device for measuring oil?
What makes a radiator lose its cool and start to boil?
Does your Big End blowing mean you can travel like the wind?
Did they create roundabouts to drive us round the bend?
Can they issue parking tickets to a stationery Mobile phone?
Can an automatic car really find its own way home?
Does spotless men you used Clearasil to wash your set of wheels?
What does being driven wild mean? Do you know how that feels?
Why do traffic lights change to red when we approach?
And traffic wardens issue tickets when no parking zones encroach?
Is panel beating for hooligans and does the winner get a cup?
Does rusty mean you're out of touch or in need of touching up?
Is reckless an addict who's injecting too much speed?
Is car theft a hobby for those children in need?
What's the difference between a joy ride and a mystery tour?
Why does Fred Flintstone drive a car without a floor?
Is a Banger a sausage or a car that's a wreck?   .
Is Whiplash for Sadists or a pain in the neck?
When a battery has lost its charge does it give its services free?
Why does it cost a fortune to pass your MOT?
If Road Tax is compulsory and Insurance another bind,
Will a Matchbox car do much damage if it strikes you from behind?
Does legless mean you're drunk or you've lost your set of wheels?
Is Fast food for the elderly and delivered on wheels as meals?
If your Exhausts exhausted is it time to go to bed?
And read Haynes manual, Highway Code or Street Map A-Z.

Tina Walker

WITHIN A GARDEN

Within a garden
Embraced by honeysuckle
Children play
Beneath the friendly apple trees:
Guardians of the garden.
Daisy chains
Lay lightly on the little heads,
While their amusements
Eddy within;
Like the recall of playground memories
Following games of *hide and seek.*
When games are over the children eat
Strawberries or nap.
Some curiously watching
Butterflies dart. Fresh start.
Embroidering their lives.
(There are no birds here)
The sun rises for a while:
The warmth of its breath
Bathing the children
In anticipation .
Of promises of play
Till moonbeams wink
To closing petals.
Within a garden.

Joyce O'Hare

A WINTER'S TALE

The day was cold.

I walked briskly on,
Until I stopped,
Suddenly,
At the pavements edge.

You stared at me,

And wrapped your arms
Around yourself . . .
Were you cold?

I looked at him,
As he sat there,
Beside you
In his ageing car

Looking smug.

I knew . . .
You'd never sat
Near him before,
Perhaps never would

Again.

Your eyes locked into mine.

We knew . . .

The day was cold,
And I walked on . . .

J E Green

WAITING IN THE WINGS
(Dedicated to Heather Holt)

If I could see your thoughts
would they tell me I'm still wanted
would they put my mind at ease
from the notion that I'm haunted
by memories of what you promised
before we were forced apart
would your thoughts still tell me
that I'm forever in your heart?

While I'm standing in the shadows
while I'm waiting in the wings
and anxiously grabbing at straws
every time the telephone rings
are you still thinking of us
and struggling to break free
from an almighty tie that binds
you to him and me?

I'm the third party in the darkness
with memories for my friends
I am only a chapter in this story
but I could help you write the end
if one day you'll call for me
and slip out of his rings
you'll bring me in from the blackness
of waiting in the wings.

Kevin Black

ON DONCASTER STATION

I'm sitting on a station
Waiting for *the* train,
I've got my plastic mac on
But I hope it doesn't rain.

We've been here for hours
My dad and me,
We've eaten all our dinner
I'm wondering what's for tea.

Is it coming yet dad?
I ask a hundredth time
'It'll be here in a minute'
We both look down the line

We've been here days!
Dad's got his camera ready,
'Can I take a photo?'
'Yes, if you hold it steady.'

Now, there's a rumble on the platform
Someone's spotted steam,
. . . but it isn't *our* train coming
I don't know *what* they've seen!

We've been here weeks!
My bottom's getting numb,
Dad looks down and smiles at me
He stops me feeling glum.

I'm sitting on a station
Waiting for a train,
But I'm out with my dad
And I'm really glad I came!

Margaret Whitehead

THE SHEPHERD

The tumbled larches let go of the sun
and the grey sheep step off their ledges
to walk the paths,
carved like wheel-ruts
among the bracken.

The shepherd turns his face to the vast sky
where the clouds are massed against the light.
Storms leave him rain-drenched and dripping
among the gnarled hawthorns
in their ancient hedgerows.

It is the wild hills, sweet with grass,
that draw him back like a green sea.
And his dog pads beside him,
as faithful as a wife.

Alison Jones

SALVE CAPUT CRUENTATUM
(O SACRED HEAD SURROUNDED)

Moisten my lips with thy sweet wine,
O my Lord, the Saviour of my soul.
Reach down with thy caring hand
From your earthly summit of crucifixion.
Touch me with thy tenderness of heart
And forgive me for my complacency.
Thou art my head, my body and my blood.
Thou, O Lord, art surrounded by those
Who are, for such a short time,
To be without their leader
And who must wait upon thy resurrection
To once again lighten their path.
O Lord, grant to us through earthly bread and wine
A share in your Heavenly benediction.

Trevor Huntington

COUCH POTATO

Couch potato, couch potato
Lounging there all day,
You're mesmerised by what you see
And always in the way.
You can't even spare the time
To change your smelly socks.
You just ignore me when I speak -
So *wrapped up* in *The Box!*
You expect your meals to be
Brought on a tray to you.
One of the few times that you move
Is to dash off to the loo
Couch potato, couch potato
I shall soon insist
You try a different kind of couch -
of a Psychiatrist!

Jim Holmes

MY LOVE FOR YOU!

From the day I found you
To this day now
My love for you
I have no doubt
Your heart and my heart
Will beat as one
As we sit here
To watch the setting of the sun
Now we are together
With love on our side
Together forever
About this I do not lie
You and me
Till the day we both die.

Trey

157

THE SNOWDROP

I look across the barren ground,
Pale Jasmine flowers against the wall,
Pink Winter Cherry floats around,
Sigh gently as they fall.

Viburnums dressed in creamy white
And Wintersweet perfumes the air,
The earth, though still and black as night,
Shelters its secrets fair.

A week goes by - I look again,
Soil still iron and bare
Another day I see - and then,
A tiny shoot is there.

'Tis time - the spring has come once more,
The snowdrop flowers are all around,
Carpeting the valley floor,
Pure white from hard, black ground.

Freda Cox

LITTLE OWL

From the wintry ash
A little owl bewitches
The silent hollows with a mournful dread.
Fine mists are spread
On hedges and in ditches
Bewildering the eye, the hand, the head.
Still, as I walk, attentive to disaster,
This guardian of silence and lone acres
Alerts my wits and what it is that masters
The soul on any pilgrimage - the dead.

Only my feet make certain what there is
And clay sticks, softening the fall
As I go home through such a wilderness
Where death swims and emptinesses call.

Alasdair Aston

EMILY

Emily is now crawling, all over the place,
Inspecting and exploring, nothing is safe
Treasured ornaments are removed,
Till she can understand, why I have to take them
From her busy little hands.

All cupboards are locked.
Such fascination they have got
More interesting than toys, lain in the toy box
She pulls herself up with any object that there
Standing proud on her tippy toes.
She hasn't a care.

She bends her knees, rocks to and fro
While she contemplates, *shall I let go,*
She jumps up and down, as if in dance
Oh! She's very clever, holding on with one hand.

The process of crawling, walking and talking
Never fails to leave me in awe
And the surprised little look
She has on her face, when bump she lands on the floor

The pleasure I feel, watching her grow
The cheeky little smile
As if she knows.

M Teal

FOG IN PLESSEY WOOD

Deep rolling fog filled Plessey Wood
      Where oak and ash and spindle stood,
Like spectral sentinels part seen
      In some ghostly evanescent dream.
And tears from weeping branches sound
      Dull muffled notes on sodden ground.
Blackwater Brook, softer still through the trees,
      Took an underground route 'neath a humus of leaves.
Ethereal and damp, like a darkening pall,
      The encircling fog settled down over all.
Not a sound could be heard till a mile off or more
      Came the indistinct snarl of a Vincent Square Four.
The listening wood seemed to follow its course
      As it gained Picket's Point and roared
On passed the gorse.
      On to Plessey, so fast, with the fog thicker still
Where the rider confused, missed the bend by Goff's Mill.
      And with elegant ease, like a skier airborne,
Both the rider and bike cleared the bordering thorn.
      Did he see in the headlight the trees as he fell?
Did he hear in the wrecking the ear-splitting knell?
      Does he care in his resting place fog - dark and still,
That the east wind is stirring o'er heathland
      And hill.

Graham Stockwell

SLEEPING IN THE ARMS OF PEACE

Don't be afraid
I am only sleeping
I hear you weep
For my rest is not deep

Don't be scared
I am not hurting
I hear you call
Yet I cannot touch you,
I fear to fall

I see a new world here
While I sleep
A beacon of inspiration
Within exists no racial segregation

Black and white join hands
With love in their hearts
A unified, enchanting team
I must be sleep drifting in
Luther King's dream.

This world seems ironic
But beautiful to me
A vision of pure harmony
That will sadly never be

Your pleading I will now entice
I shall wake now
I am blessed, I have
Witnessed paradise.

Nina Ramm

TURKEY

I used to run around all day,
keeping all the chicks at bay,
But then the farmer caught me,
Oh no! I'm to be his tea!
I thrashed and kicked and again I thrashed,
But *Bonk!* The farmer I've bashed.
I tried to escape but he's too quick,
Gobble, gobble, gobble began a little chick,
A commotion, a commotion I said,
But alas I got a bash on the head!
I think I am dead,
And I fall like lead,
Onto the solid ground,
With a very loud sound!
I am stripped of my feathers,
Which were soft as heather,
My head's chopped off and so are my feet,
I've got to be cooked for them to eat.
I go on the tray and into the oven,
Ow! It's so hot, I've got to be jumpen!
Oh my God! Oh by gum!
Out of the oven I now come,
Roast potatoes now by me,
Now it's time for their tea!
They cut me up into chunks,
I want to be outside with all those hunks!

Laura Jones (12)

THE PATIENT'S LAMENT - A DIRGE

Oh! Lack a day! Oh dear! I wist
We patients have upset the receptionists
Because on Monday we cannot foretell
That on Wednesday we'll awake feeling very unwell

Before daybreak we're roused from our slumber
By drums in our head that are dancing a Rumba
With a fevered brow and a churning tum
We wait endless hours for the dawn to come

At 8.30 sharp we reach for the phone
Oh! The number's engaged; well we might have known
We keep on trying until it's 10.30
Our temperature's rising and we're getting shirty

So to the Medicine Man's House we wend our way
And pray for an appointment by the end of the day
'The doctor you need' You're informed with aplomb
'Will see you next Friday at 11.21.

'It's the earliest possible' you are told with scant sorrow
'You certainly can't see him this time tomorrow'
You groan your condition can't endure such a wait
But the time and the date are inviolate

So it's back to our bedroom and we hope Nirvana
And trust that we'll wake at this time mañana
So if smiling faces are yearned for by Gill
Why the heck does she work with folks who are ill?

J D Baines

NO HOPE - (A CALL FOR HELP)

In this land of want and need,
people starve and cannot feed.
There is no food so they have no greed,
they're land to dry to grow a seed.

Greedy horse flies busy flying
as naked bodies sit there dying,
a mother watching helplessly sighing
as her, starving baby, lies there crying.

The future's black as black as night,
Their strength has gone they have no fight,
Their hope for life has gone from sight,
Will no-one help them through their plight.

Keith Jones

SCHOOL

I wish that I'd tried harder,
While I was still at school,
Learned more of maths and English,
Instead I played the fool,
You need an education,
Are the words that I was told,
Try harder while you're still a child
Too late once you grow old.
I wouldn't listen to them,
I thought that I knew best,
Who needs maths and English,
Who needs their silly test
But now that I am older,
And wiser grown by far,
How I wish that I had listened,
No job! No cash! No car!

John Pressley

ENDANGERED SPECIES

The dancing candle flame
Leaps to and fro in feverish battle,
But, in one blow, the delicate
Flicker of life is snuffed out
By the destructive touch of man.

Man was put on this earth
To protect the innocent, defend the weak,
Yet the traitor, facing the almighty
Power of the trusting whale
And the fragility of the seal pup,
Senselessly strikes the fatal blow
Time and time and time again.

How does it feel to deny their right
To swamp the bamboo-scattered forests
Or grace the African plains with life?
No miracle can return the black and white
Creatures to the very root of existence,
As their sorrowful eyes, weeping with fear,
Reflect pound and dollar signs,
The flash of a blade and barrel of a gun.

Soon it will be too late.
Too late to reunite the mother with her baby,
Too late to remove the wounding bullet
Or flesh-ripping harpoon.
Too late to breathe life
Into a textbook colour photograph.

Michelle Hurst

LYCANTHROPY

Skin tingling, twitching, eyes begin smarting
Burning, nerve ends searing, a change is starting
Heightened senses, smell and sight
The tell tale lunar glow of night
Clothes discarded, torn from flesh
As limbs disjoin then reform, remesh
Coarse dark hair disseminates the form
Of the four legged creature now being born
Feet and hands once human, now paws
Nails extending like talons, no, claws!
Canine teeth growing, jaws dislocate
Mind filled with fear, agony and hate
A ripping of skin as the snout elongates
Distending ears twitching in wolf like traits
Spine twisting, bending and the final aversion
Brain and body now lupine, no longer a person
A growl and snarl, the baring of teeth
Metamorphosis to werewolf is almost complete
Hackles erect as it paces the room
With a strange compulsion to howl at the moon
Tail swishes down in a powerful arc
As the hind legs launch the beast at the dark
The craving, the hunger for the human fruit
To satiate the appetite of this formidable brute
Man will for life and sanity grope
When faced with the curse of the Lycanthrope

Steffan Blaidd

BARBARIAN

The barbarian stands impatient to conquer
Despite all impossible odds
As the ficklers of fortune panic
And are selling their wealth for new Gods

And bleeding and bloody the blows of war
As bruised and battered you die
But virtue and valour can never be slain
Strong belief in the look of an eye

The foe outshadow the horizon
And a gloom replaces blue sky
And you really believe that if you must
Then this is the place to die

The trumpeters sally forward
And the drummers begin their beat
And now is for going forward
To the midst of the dusty heat

You're there in the middle of battle
Alone save yourself against them
And gored you fight on remorseless
Man against man against men

Then it is suddenly over
And the dust starts to fall away
As grown men call out for their mothers
And the children begin to pray

The odds were always in favour
Paths of truth have never been lost
But what a waste in all this haste
Of the lives of the many who lost

Frank Samet

BROTHERS

It is hard to express sometimes
I think you have what I am looking for in life
A spice perhaps not in my veins, from a spirit of ancients
Perhaps a time I missed, a wisdom I do not possess
I think you live as you feel, not how you should in the eyes of them
A child, I remember at a classroom window, boastful of behaviour
You and him walking, tall, apart
Not dressed the way you should
You as a man I am not
Just a changing situation
We were always a pair, you two, the lads, my boys, my sons,
Two brothers.

Stefan John Rodgers

AUTUMN IN HOPWAS WOODS, NEAR TAMWORTH

Tip-toe into the woodland
Stand on a bed of wet soggy leaves,
Smell the earthy smell of the woodland floor,
Rub your hands on the bark of the trees.
Feel the roughened texture of the oak tree,
The smooth grey green bark of the beech
Touch the luminous papery bark of the graceful silver birch.
Up to the spiky green brown encased conkers on the horse
                                        chestnut tree reach
Gaze enraptured at the red, white spotted Fly Agaric,
Rivel up your nose at the pongy odour of the drab Stink Horn,
Look at the scarlet, rounded, clustered rowan berries
Moulded in such a glowing translucent form.
Tip-toe out of the woodland
Away from the earthy smell of the wet, soggy leaves
Into the brilliant ray of an autumn gold sunshine's glow,
But remember deep in your heart the touch,
And scents of so many different toadstools and trees.

Vivian Khan

BLACKBALLED

It was a very attractive house,
In the pleasant little market town:
The rooms were clean, the food was good,
The guests in the lounge quietly settling down -
> But not the American.

With typical English reticence,
Talking to no-one, they quietly at,
Idly look at magazines,
Never chattering of *this and that* -
> Except the American.

She turned to her husband for confirmation
Of all that she said, and the poor little clot,
Called Sam, but obviously *Uncle* to no-one,
Had to agree, that he'd much rather not -
> Though he, too, was American.

In self-defence they all went to bed,
Tired of hearing her life's full story.
They made their excuses - 'Packing to do,'
'Big day ahead,' Very tired, so sorry,' -
> And left the American.

After breakfast next day, as they stood in the hall,
She struck up a pose on the stairs. 'Say, Sam,
Guess I'll just go and clean my teeth
Before I go to Birming-*ham*'
> Said the loud-voiced American

It took every bit of their English reserve
Not to burst into laughter there on the spot,
But it melted the ice as nothing else could,
And by common consent they agreed they could not
> Accept that American.

Margaret Leith Shaw

169

ALONE IN A CROWDED ROOM

Alone in a crowded room,
The silence in my head
The heavy weight upon my eyes,
Like a massive tonne of lead.

The door is constantly breathing,
The paper is busy talking.
The computer is quietly humming,
And pairs of feet are walking.

I sit quietly at my desk,
And stare into space.
My head begins to throb,
As I clamp my hands on my face.

I'm in darkness now,
In my own little room.
Light is pouring through the windows,
Like the light from the moon

This day will end I hope,
I hope it ends real soon.
I don't like being here,
Alone in a crowded room.

Eifion Thomas

THE GOLDEN ROSE

A golden rose I give to you,
　upon a winter's morn,
A golden rose I give to you,
　a rose without a thorn.

And if this rose so shiny bright,
　were worth its weight in gold,
It could not be the worth, the love for you,
　within my heart I hold.

A golden rose I give to you,
  upon a winter's morn,
and I wish you love, and peace and joy,
  once more, this Christmas morn.

Bernadette Fitzharris

LIVERPOOL REVISITED

If home is where the heart is
This is where I belong.
In this cathedral of scousers
And of soccer and song.
On the streets of a city
Which knows trouble and strife,
A place Carl Jung proclaimed
As: *The Pool of Life.*
Long since left locations
Resume familiarity of form
As Liverpool is again
My shelter from the storm.
From the Town Hall to the High Street.
That traverses Wavertree,
Down to the docks and Dingle
That flank old man Mersey.
Up to the icon that's Anfield
And the glow that's Everton
Makes a return of nostalgia
For a prodigal son
Who left long ago
For a *better-life* elsewhere
And missed out on the vibes
In the Liverpool air.

David Cassidy

DO SOMETHING

Nobody either really matters either . . .
She says she could give up everything
Not miss it.
There is not a great lot to carry on for . . .

The pain she had
I don't blame her.
But what can she do to cease it?

Her husband has left her.
A forestry worker.
They lived way out
In the country.

Nothing to do
Nothing to see.
Except wood.
For the trees.

She's desperate
She's lonely
Aw . . .
God . . .

Do something!

J Duel-Crake

BALLOONS

Balloons balloons are very, very pretty.
Balloons balloons are very, very shiny.
You can punch them you can kick them.
You can whack them, you can smack them.
You can do all sorts of things with a balloon,
Because it's a balloon, it's a balloon.

David Owens (8)

WHAT'S A FELLA TO DO?

That little knob looks interesting -
  I wonder what it does?
I think perhaps I'll try . . .
  Oh! All it does is buzz!
Now you wouldn't think that that
  Would get mummy so upset,
Never mind, s'pose I'll go and get
  This - ooh! What can it be?
Only know it feels smashing to me.
It's funny stuff that makes you sneeze
  Oh! Won't someone tell me please,
What is pepper I'd like to know,
  P'raps I'll find out when I grow.
Dear me - what's a fella to do
  When he is not quite two!

Here comes mummy once again,
  She's come to bring my little train,
Not half as interesting as this -
  This is absolute sheer bliss.
'It's daddy's wrist watch' comes a yell -
Well how on earth was I to tell?
What's a wrist watch I'd like to know?
  P'raps I'll find out when I grow,
Dear me - what's a fella to do
  When he is not quite two!

Sheila Richardson

GUESS WHO?

Before you've written off TV
Just wish for one you'd love to see;
Better than all who's been before,
And certainly worth waiting for.

Imagine one came down from heaven,
Was on your TV screen at seven;
A programme never to forget,
Compulsive viewing on your set.

And present in the studio,
Are characters of long ago;
People from every rank and file,
Are greeted with a friendly smile.

A reader stands with book in hand,
Tells stories of another land;
He turns the pages and he reads,
Of miracles and kindly deeds.

From the New Testament he'd read,
And then he turned to one and said:
'Your love is everlasting rife,
Lord Jesus Christ - This is your life.'

Raymond Young

DEAREST CHILD

You made of me a shape so ungainly before you were born,
Inflicted pain whilst toe-tapping on my rib cage,
Practising for the dance to come.

Technicolor was apt for the emergence of such a star;
Glorious hues of lilac, purple, crimson and white,
Birth colours unappreciated at the time.

Then, soft-furred and warm like a ripe apricot,
I nibbled and you nuzzled, mutually absorbing
And inhaling odour and ardour.

I clung on to this image of you during the black time -
Trying to hide the memory of your hateful stares
When you were lost in defiant rebellion.

I covered over those thoughts with marshmallow innocence,
Tried to shut out the black of your mouth, hair, soul -
Coloured you rachel, pink and white.

Divided by our sameness we are twinned but not attuned,
And oh, the outpourings, pride and shame enjoined.
Such excesses of emotion expended - remembered.

But womanhood bestows its serape of assumed serenity,
Enfolding a cloak of maturity around the young girl
Though she hides the vixen and bids her *stay.*

And now my child with child, I feel again the magnetism
Of giving loving nurture and existence to another being,
Regeneration of self, the ultimate expression.

Barbara Graham

THE QUIET PLACE

In the hectic rush of modern life
When speed alone seems King,
And men give scarce a second thought
For any other thing,
How few will slow this frenzied pace
To find within - the quiet place.

With tempers frayed, and nerves stretched taut,
They seek so hard to wrest
The last mad moment from each hour,
Then find they've missed the best,
The peace that's theirs by God's good grace,
The calm within - the quiet place.

Oh, stay awhile, and learn anew
To ease this harassed mind,
Give time to look with tranquil eyes
On beauty one can find
When one has ceased this frantic race,
And finds with joy - the quiet place.

B M Andrews .

THANK YOU FROM YOUR FRIEND OF THE SEA

You've cried a million tears for me
And made this salty sea
It's peaceful here, it's tranquil here
We live in harmony.

There is no war or hate or shame
Just our dolphin pride
For we are the friends of all beings
We sailors of the tide.

Tell me why you weep young child
Come stay with me, be free and wild
Leave your world of trouble and toil
Mankind's feet are stuck steadfast in the soil.

Let our spirits never be enslaved
A lifetime dancing with the waves.

Kim Harrison

THE THING

What is this thing I see before me
Laying prostrate on the floor?
I've been in the room several times
It wasn't there before.
I've poked it and I've prodded it,
Examined every inch,
I've shouted out, and stamped my feet
It didn't even flinch.
I don't know what to do with it
I've not see the like before,
Should I hang it from the ceiling?
Or nail it to the door?
I've thumbed through the encyclopaedia
From A right through to Z,
But couldn't find a mention
Of that thing beside the bed.
I've thought until my brain hurt,
Until I can think no more,
I really don't know what it is
But my God, it looks sore.

Brenda George

BEYOND

Beyond this dream of night and day,
Beyond all mortal ken;
Beyond this place of time and space
Could there be *someone* then?
Beyond this blue of sky and earth,
Beyond this shadowed dream,
Around the darkest hour,
Does a light to guide us gleam?
Beyond our world and all the rest,
Beyond these things all fashioned,
Bound up with law and order,
Don't tell me it all just happened.
Beyond this life and grim dark death,
Beyond its grief, its care,
Beyond this den of imprisoned men,
There *must* be someone there.

John Clarkson Taylor

A SILENT WORLD

A silent world is
an exciting place
because your eyes
turn into ears
and your ability to smell
becomes your ability to hear.
Vibrations give you messages
enabling you to hear.
Your hands do the talking,
sending messages through
both pictures and writing.
So now you can see a
Silent world without noise
is noisy in other ways.

Rose-Ann Omalley

SOMEWHERE

Somewhere there's a curlew call
Across a purple moor,
A rugged snow-capped mountain,
The view of a distant shore.

Somewhere a wood is waking
To bird-song and wild flower,
While the cuckoo on its borrowed nest
Awaits its finest hour.

Somewhere a rainbow arches
The ashen rain-washed skies
As shafts of sunlight lance green hills
In an azure of surprise.

Somewhere there's a spiralling lark
Above a field of corn -
A summer morning shining
In a radiance of dawn.

Somewhere a flower-flecked meadow
Dreams in the noon-day sun,
Where sleeps my land of lost content
Three score years on.

Somewhere, there's a white road
Winding to the sea -
Here silence speaks in crooning waves
To a harmony of memory.

Somewhere deep in the human heart
Hope springs eternal:
Each springtime, every Easter,
Time's abiding miracle.

Eileen King

VE

A hope and a dream, lives in the night,
A vision of life, without having to fight,

        Bang! It collapses,
        The sirens are on,
        People are crying,
        Man dies with the bomb.

Cheated of chance, bitter with pain,
Hope still remains,
The dream grows again,

Faith in the people, who know the strength,
Know how to fight, women and men,
The fear's not of dying but of failing to save,
A world they remember
        and dream will come again.

Faye L Barker

ODE TO A WORM

There once was a house
In which lived a mouse
In which lived a worm
And the worm did squiggle and squirm.

The mouse grew thin
The worm grew stout
And then one day
The mouse -
He passed away
And the worm
passed
out.

Lyndsay Currie

DECEPTION

No, you're wrong, it can't be true,
I refuse to believe your claim,
They're weeds you're planting in my flowerbed,
You've complete misplaced the blame,
The one deceiving is you.
Pump decaying thoughts into my head,
Suggesting emotions are buried and dead,
These destructive roots strangle me,
But I resist the force knowing it can't be.
I would have known by now if you were right,
In what you're telling me,
Our future together is clear and bright,
I'll turn and from your words flee.
No, you're wrong it can't be true,
The one deceiving is you.

A L Hicks

MORNING SONG

I hold this image in my inmost mind,
On the canvas of my soul encaptured,
A transient moment, when one sometimes finds
Breathing stops and hearts can pause, enraptured.
I break the trance and leave the magic place
And hasten to record that fragile flush
Of dawn, when colour bridges time and space.
I am no painter, words must be my brush.

The mists of morning harmonise the land
And pink-tinged slates reflect a river's gleam.
Familiar objects, touched by unseen hand
Transmuted into jewels, as in dream.
The vision flickers, dies, in daytime's shroud,
Eludes my grasp, unclutchable as cloud.

Margaret Wycherley

AFTER HILLSBOROUGH

'You'll never walk alone,' they sang
     and the neighbours rallied round
As they laid their hats and scarves and flowers
     at their favourite football ground
'Abide with Me,' the crowds all sang
     and it echoed across the land
But many never knew the touch
     of the Father's loving hand.

The people stood in silence
     and wept for the ones who died
And the ones who were still in hospital
     and the mothers and fathers who cried.
'Tear down the barriers!' people said
     'It must never happen again.'
But they knew no peace in their grieving hearts
     As they stood in the street in the rain.

They didn't remember the reason why
     the barriers first went up
To separate the warring fans
     As they cheered their teams to the Cup.
Old rivals stood together there,
     no red or blue today
Only a love for each other now,
     but what a price to pay.

God's love would bring them comfort
     if they prayed 'Abide with me,'
For God's love know no barriers
     and His gift of salvation is free,
And those verses sung in sincerity
     as many a Christian has known
Will truly bring God's peace because
     we never walk alone.

Elizabeth Thurgood

MOTHER

Mother don't leave me now
My insecurity will arrive
I don't think I could survive
Dad has passed away
Please don't pass me by
Married siblings have moved away
Married wife and kids have gone astray
Mother don't leave me now
My insecurity will arrive
I don't think I could survive
The devil's brew might arrive
Mother please stay a while
Ask God your friend to let me go
To where it is I must go
Let him let you let me
Beat the devil's brew
Then I will survive
Mother! Mother!
Please don't leave me now
My insecurity will arrive
I don't think I could survive
Mother the devil's brew arrived
But thanks to you he did not stay
At your going away to dad to stay
Came my siblings to bye to say
Came my wife and kids to bye to say
Came your friend a while
Mother I will survive the while
Your friend I asked to stay the while.

Carson Scott

JUST THE POST?

On tenterhooks I wait for you, with anticipation I listen,
When I wake, the thought of you brings hope, something new,
Fresh air may be my engine but you are my piston,
You arrive with my mid day breaks and the morning dew,
Mr Postman, it's you.

The dog barks, the letter box raps, eager I bound down the stairs,
Is it for me? Is it for me? Thoughts swirl as I pounce at the door,
The excitement, the thrill, the knowledge that someone cares,
As you relieve my loneliness, my spirits soar,
Mrs Postman it's you.

In this world full of despair, upset and distress,
Where no-one has nice things to say,
I turn to you for good tidings and from my sadness, a rest,
I long for your visits each day,
Master Postman, it's you.

But some days you don't come and empty is the floor,
Empty is the inspiration, that hope and imagination,
There's no possibilities, no roots for change - not like before,
When fresh air was my engine and you were my piston,
Miss Postman, it's you.

L J Simkins

THE LIVING-DEAD ESSENCE OF LIFE

Water is a dead killer,
For itself is not alive.
As this vital murderer,
Plunges up and down,
We must think of the life it gives,
The life it makes,
The life it takes.

But it is not entirely to blame,
We pollute it,
We die because of it.
Fish die because of us.
We should also be on trial.
We drink our own poison.

So as you drink this living-dead,
Think of the bitter bed,
Of its home, the river
The living-dead essence of life.

Jonny Evans (12)

TEARDROPS

Teardrops in the sand
  As I watch, and wait for you
I know you won't be coming
  Today, the truth I knew
You've left me for another
  What was it, I did wrong?
I'd given up my heart
  I thought our love was strong
My life now seems so empty
  With you, not by my side
Oh how my heart is breaking
  My tears, I try to hide
I'll watch the waves come lapping
  Upon the sandy beach
They'll swallow all my teardrops
  And take them out of reach
No teardrops to remind me
  Of a love I had and lost
But memories can't be taken
  My heart will pay the cost.

Linda Robertson

MY WRITING

I sit in my van with paper and pen
And write down my thoughts of women and men
Some are memories of my boyhood and youth
Some are quite funny but all tell the truth.
I've written down poems and odes about friends
I've written about strikes and political trends
But all of this matters not one little bit
'Cos it's all for my pleasure and my own benefit.
You see I'm embarrassed and basically shy
About writing my poetry and I do not know why
I cannot explain these feelings I hold
So I write them down so they will be told.

I used to think it was silly to write all the time
To put down my thoughts and ideas all in rhyme
Till Christmas came and I had a wee drink
And I came to realise it's the way that I think
And the friends at my work liked what I wrote
So I decided to *come out* and grab the world by the throat
I'm still not sure of how I will take
To being told that a poet I never will make
But for the time being I will continue to be
The guy who writes poems for parties and *me*.

J M Govan

THE THREAD AND WEB FLY

The ducks startled the water in the glinting sun
Poppies burst, their memory an explosion
Distorting beauty, old cold pain freed
Out into the sunlight, alive again.

Robbing the children, who ran scared and shrieking
Trying to hold on while mother cried in a heap
Puzzling hosts.

But through the eye's mist and sky's mist
Of cool white haze, a tree's horizon of love's common-sense.
And the blue thread and web of the fly
Appeared and disappeared.

A barn, stirring up much deeper childhood shame
Recalled a kind of pentimento:
Past and present hanging still in the sunlight.

Tears may roll, but stubborn common-sense can
Hold still and clear a space for love.

E McKeever

ROAD RAGE

Sitting in the Wine Bar watching the world go by
As I sit I ponder and I wonder why
They rush around like mad men with never a moment to think
Never time to say 'Hello, mate, would you like a drink?'

And then there is the motorist
Now, there's the strangest fellow!
He drives around at breakneck speed
And you'll hear him bellow
'What do you think you're doing,
You ignorant, stupid fool?'

If only he would calm down
And regain his cool!

Then he'd realise the truth
That speed can drive you mad
It really can distort the mind
Now, that is really sad!

He thinks he rules the highways
He things he knows it all
But one day he will realise
That he is *the ignorant fool*!

Stephen Friede

NIGHT THOUGHTS

When I lie in bed at night with all the lights off,
I pull the covers over my head,
And just think about things,
Any old things like . . .
I'm in a high speed racing car racing against Michael Schumacher
And I'm turning the last bend with Schumacher behind, way behind in
                                                    the pits and I win!
But soon I'm not in a racing car, I'm in armour fighting Goblins
                                                    and Dragons,
Next I'm bungy jumping off Mount Everest,
Then I'm parachuting from a plane,
But I think it's much safer turning on the light and reading!

David Lewis Evans (10)

ROSE OF LOVE

I'm enchanted by the rose,
The splendid rose of love,
The symbol of desire,
That sets the hearts on fire,
With ecstasy and emotion,
Once given with devotion,
The crimson velvet flower,
Has magic love and power,
Once given by your lover,
There could never be another,
That could ever say so much,
Your heart it's sure to touch.
It's only if you part,
Then the thorns will pierce your heart,
Treat your rose with care,
Then its love is yours to share.

Caroline Robinson

WELL-WISHER

When tripping sunshine found the rare
And secret autumn in your hair,
And shared the disclosed cache with me,
It was no joy, and no surprise:
For though I'd loved you quite, withal;
More docile than a man should be;
Long swayed by you in winsome thrall;
The word was to the weary wise
And well-aware -
Though but a twilight ceorl
To you, my brittle jewel.

You never knew that, in the bare
Recesses of my chamber, where
I grew swift-disabused to see
The two-way mirror of your eyes;
My past adjured me to recall
Stale airs that cried, like yours, 'Me! Me!'
Precursors of a seasoned fall
That I'd long learned to recognise.
So, take good care;
But what a sly, slight girl
Are you: why, little fool?

Suzanne Bowes

SPRING TIME

Spring time, birds singing, flying to and fro
Animals collecting twigs and straw, they seem to know
Spring is here, everywhere, trees and plants burst into green.
The trees wake, from their wintry sleep.
With outstretched arms, nearly touching the sky.
Buds bursting forth, on the branches so high.
Flowers pop up their sleepy heads.
Awoken from their wintry beds.
Oh! What a pretty sight is this.
Spring is here, what a bliss.
The buds on the trees, burst their sleepy heads
Opening forth, their leaves so green.
Everywhere, now starts to look serene.
Hedgerows come to life, again, they breathe.
Trees stand tall and proud.
Now they have their emerald crown.
Majestically they wave their outstretched arms.
As the breeze gently blows the boughs
The sun breaks through their quivering leaves
Now each tree stands so portly and calm, each flower
Gently sways in the breeze
As all things, settle back to enjoy the spring.

P Armishaw

UNDER THE GLOW

Movement in shadow
I stare, in the glow
Of the sodium lamp
Into a time long ago
Here in this street
Where love was first shown
Are shadows of people
Are memories in stone
Here on this pavement
With my heart in my head
Echoes of time
Resurrecting the dead

So here I step
Into a time long ago
Chasing the shadows
In the sodium glow
Here are my memories
In the amber of night
Ghost of the past
Living in life
Here on this pavement
Under the glow
I haunt the steps
Of a child's life, long ago.

D C S Childs

A LITTLE LIFE IN THE SUBURBS

She sits in front of the tele and watches it all day long.
The *old man* sits in the garden shed, as he dreams of the times now gone.
She does not really see it, not the news, the soaps, the strife.
He does not like it much in the shed, but it's better than the company of
his *beloved wife.*

He loved her once, or so he says but now he's not so sure.
She says that she has never loved him, now he is just a *bore.*
All the things that they once knew, are dead, buried deep in the past.
Happiness, contentment was fleeting, for sure it did not last.
Their children come to see them, call around to clean the house.
She very rarely speaks to them, the *old man* sits in his shed like a mouse.
She does not actually see them as they move about her chair.
They try hard to get her to talk to them, in her mind she is not there.
Her memory is a forgotten song,
She sits in her chair all day long.
Sometimes she does not know their name,
It is *old age dementia,* there's no-one to blame.
God grant your mercy, give them the light,
For one brief moment restore their sight.
Two lonely people locked away,
Apart from each other from day to day.
Restore the dignity they once knew,
Than take them Lord, they belong to you.

E C Mulligan

IVY

Cold ivy, supported -
Trying to strangle the last life,
Dead root and alien.
A systematic killer,
Pleasant to the eye
In some time-honoured way.
A stump allowing all that is living
To weave its way from hell
But, being hastened in its own demise,
Refuses access to freedom
And poison snarls its way back
Searching for another,
More living host.

Reg Sealey

OUR STREET

I like the street I live in
It's full of history
All its streets are named
To do with monasteries

We have *Abbots Way* and
Friars Walk even got a *Monks Close*
With *Edwards Ave, Montford Place*
But *Abbots Way*, I love the most

Someone once told me
That tunnels run under our feet.
Just think of all the history
That went on in *our street!*

Patricia Belfield

PET WORLD

Life sold here for less than a Blockbuster video. Chew on a Mars or any
sweetie for sale by the in-door as you ogle the panorama of living merchandise.
Andrex puppies and calendar pin-up kittens, displayed in
ethnic order in spartan booths - fluffy arcade game toys inviting your wallet
to score - aah. Is the pet you've already bought a coy cage squatter - soiling
its food tray, side-stepping its bells and other made-in-Macau playthings?
- fancy something slimier? Watch pubescent fast-food faces lead you with
acne grins to velvet spiders or long-tongued lizards - real McCoy exotica for
your lounge. Let rainbow selections of plastic paraphernalia arouse your
latent design flair and help you create a back-to-nature habitat. Make sure it's
camouflaged into the MFI Boxing Day bargain nesting in your living room.
Check out dinky cage kits in co-ordinated pastels for your take-aways too. Kits
for kids who need hamsters come in lurid purples and petrol blues to match
Fisher Price or Lego sets, and to throwaway as you outgrow them - if you're
green, they even upgrade like your mum's computer. Hunt out complete
aquariums in Ikea style pre-packs - ready to receive struggling, squirming fish
fished out of luminous fin-packed Pet World tanks and into handy plastic bags
- till-bound. Not Dixons or Do-it-All, It's Pet World. What commercial beauty
- bountiful parthogenic stock. An at arms' length computer delete - the only
record of damaged goods. My new toy feels warm in its cardboard box, paid
mine by plastic. En-route to my customised nest, I'll let it take a de-tour to
Tesco's for my weekly shopping.

Daphne Kasriel

QUIETLY, THE MOMENT GREW DIM

Quietly, she awoke from her malaise
Momentarily distracted from her days
of sadness and abuse from him
then just as swift the moment grew dim.

Returned to the darkness of her life
of selflessness and abuse as a wife,
she staggered towards the cupboard door
and fell ragdoll-like to the floor.

Roland Glover

QUICK! HIDE THE WELCOME MAT!

You've probably met the type before -
The moment they walk in the door
Their eyes are going everywhere.
You show them politely to a chair
Then find they've followed to the kitchen,
Where you're making coffee and they're itching
To inspect every little cranny and nook,
Nothing escapes their hawk-like look.
They are experts at *damning with faint praise*
And one of their less endearing ways
Is to say in tones that drip with ice,
'Oh, yes, - it really looks *quite* nice.'
While all the time they chatter madly
About their *friends,* and how badly
Their health has been - how they suffer!
No-one ever has had life rougher,
And battle, murder and sudden death
Whilst scarcely pausing to draw breath.
Why do they think that they're the one
To advise on how things *should* be done?
I feel that murder and sudden death will be
Theirs - and it will be done by me!

Joan Weston

THE SEASONS

The freshness of the Spring
On a quiet Sunday morning
When a distant church bells ring
And new-born lambs
Their first steps take
God's new born lands
With sweet new life awake

The beauty of the summer
With skies of sunny blue
Gardens filled with roses
And flowers, of every hue
With laughing happy children
On golden, sandy shores
The green and yellow patchwork of the fields
Who on Earth, could ask for more.

The glory of the Autumn
When leaves begin to fall
And golden yellow shades
Take on a new delightful form
The amber of the sunset
At the closing of the day
The harvest all is gathered
And safely stored away.

The first nip of Winter
As frost bites the air
Robins perch on holly branches
And carols, rent the air
White snowflakes, gently falling
Tell us Winter
Once more is here

Irene G Corbett

MEN

They are there when you need them
They are there when you don't
They make life worth living
And then they don't
They say that they love you
Then they say that they never did
They say that they hate you
Then you wonder why they do
They say you're confused
When you know it's really them
They tell you that you're wonderful
Then they say that you're horrible
Then they say that you're sexy
Then say it was a lie
You say that they were nasty
Then they say that they're not
You say they can't tell the truth
They say that they can
They tell you when they want you
They need you to love them
They need you to hold them
They need you to nurse them
They need you to laugh with them
They need you to cry with them
They need you to play with them
They need you to make their dinner
They need you to be at home for them
But most of all
They are there when you need them
And they are there when you don't

Lynda Forsyth

BLACK COUNTRY AS ERS SPOKE

Owd Ali wos fedup a livin
he wus sick with a pairn in is yed.
on frittened to step airta bed like
just in cairse he drapped darrrn jed.
sew he sent fer is missis ode Martha
ood wunce bin a right cumly wench
on er saw he'd slept wi is socks on
on accaarnt o the orrible stench.
Er stood theer un bawled aart at Eli
Yo know wots up wi yoor yed
Yo'm askin fer trouble wi ye socks on
why do yer tak em off, like I sed.
If yo'n wore um a day yo'm wore em a wick
on they' stinking the ouse summat shockin
Yo cun just tak em off, on meck it right quick
on yo'll find that yer yed soon stops nockin.
So sure as er spoke Ali's yedairk just went
on e jumped aarta bed wi a shout
E chatted up Martha un borryed the rent
on went dairn tew the Pub fer a stout.

which just guster proove, if yo ai gorra bean
un cor raise the price of a drink
wer yer socks fer a wick, on yer Missus'l pay
if just to get rid o the stink.

Norman Taylor

ODE TO LOVE AT 60+

With railcard to hand and overnight bag
I boarded the InterCity
'Cos I was off for a four hour trip
With no man in tow
More's the pity!
I was dressed quite well
In my nicest suit
My face a bit wrinkly and old
But I sat myself down
And got out my book
Which was really *hot stuff* I'd been told
A gent sat beside me
And started to chat
About nothing particular
Just this and that
The journey was long and at times very slow
So we found ourselves talking with more of a flow
He was widowed and sixty and visiting his son
For him, as for me, journey's end was Brighton
He had a kind face and a very nice smile
Been retired from the Bank for quite a long while
He asked about me, where I lived, what I did
We warmed to each other so well
Was this love at first sight
I thought to myself
Or just me under British Rail's spell?
The journey was over, we smiled, we shook hands
And both went our separate ways
I watched him walk off and thought -
Not love, you old fool, just too many TV plays!

Sheila Edwards

THE COMPUTER HAS ASSUMED TOO MUCH . . .

I'm a microchip computer with an electronic mind:
I'm held in very high regard tho' sometimes much maligned;
No wonder I'm deflated - my performance underrated -
A sophisticate intelligence not of the human kind.

I'm a microchip computer with an automatic brain:
I'm fed with the wrong data but it's me that takes the blame;
My intellect's insuperable, my memory indisputable -
A master-mind, created from a scientific dream.

I'm a microchip computer, I was born without a soul,
I hear you're working on it but you won't achieve this goal:
Fashioned from technology - I can't *do* sociology -
Personal relations does not fall within my role.

I'm a microchip computer and your wish is my command,
And tho' I'll do my best for you, to meet all your demands,
Questions in profusion only lead to my confusion;
Please be more specific or you'll surely blow my mind.

I'm a microchip computer but I cannot stand the pace:
It was never my desire to join this world's atomic chase;
So when you finally press my key don't stare with incredulity -
It was not my decision to destroy the human race.

Cynthia M Oliver

WHO AM I?

I'm not a leggy green-eyed blonde (although I'd *like* to be)
The sight of me on a nudist beach would make the seagulls flee,
Squeezing blobby bits into size 14 jeans gets me in a stew,
And my sagging cleavage no longer does - what *I* want it to!

I'm a working mother, juggling a career, with house, interests, and family
And I've gained the odd achievement that I thought was probably beyond me,
I'm over-emotional, well - I still blubber at *Little House on the Prairie* -
And I find looking in the mirror now, an experience that's scary!

My passions are poetry, country music, dolphins, sunsets and snow
I believe we're all here for a purpose, and mine I'd like to know.
I try to be helpful and genuine, and show people that I care -
But I must admit, I do scream, when I find yet *another* white hair!

I drive everyone mad, with my miniature cottages' collection.
I'm not politically aware - unless *I* was running for election!
I can't do crosswords, or sew, or cook, or knit -
In fact, if you hadn't met me, you'd think I was a half-wit!

Like everyone, I have worries, and wonder if life is passing me by,
And to say I don't have unrealistic dreams, would only be a lie,
I do the pools, and occasional *flutter* but am not overloaded with money -
And I drive around in a *flintstone* car, that is forever going *funny*!

I think of my secure job, lovely kids, nice house, good husband and things
And realise that *these* are my treasures, as I count my blessings,
So I guess being happy in yourself must surely be the key -
Then 'Who am I' becomes Mrs Contented - and that will do for me!

Lynda Miller

MEMORIES OF NICHOLAS (NICK)

Dear Nick so many times I think of you and cry
Why at so young an age did you have to die?
I think back over the years, the happy times we shared
I think of the work you did for others, how you cared
I try to be happy, but so often I'm blue
The reason being I cannot stop thinking of you!
Whenever I see geese flying in the sky
I think of you Nick and again I cry

You were so full of life, to be with such fun
A dearly loved brother, a caring son
Your love of the Arts, and nature too
Happy and lovely dreams I have of you
Your wonderful smile, your eyes so blue

We will always remember you with love and pride
Your endless works for Charities, you took in your stride
We know you would wish us to be happy not sad
You are in a better place Nick so we must be glad!
You were so very talented and so very clever
But Nick in our hearts you will live for *ever!*

Elaine M Jordan

SOFTLY, SOFTLY

Softly, softly, as the steam pierces the gloom,
The gentle tempo matching my heartbeat.
But the iron horse, now closer draws its breath,
As loud as the thunder, now in my chest,
wishing to break free
Yet, rooted to the spot, unable to flee.
The cloud of steam covers me through
as from my hat escapes a strand of hair
I've waited too long - I no longer care.
A hiss of brakes, a shudder of metal
  - carriage doors crash open
  hob nailed boots clatter
  I stand and stare.
Then through the crowd - a familiar gaze
As towards me he does race
  reaches out- caresses my face
and gently moves the strand of hair
  and shyly looks into my eyes.
For patience rewarded - my turn has come,
Back from the war - my soldier
                    We won!

C A Statham

ABSENCE

A grey morning.
No sunshine.

She follows the dogs' gaze to the emptiness
At the top of the spiral stair
Where he used to appear, head down,
Fair hair brushing the step
Each morning.

Dogs padding after, she wanders the house.
Sitting room. Calm, orderly.
No cushions piled on the floor for trampolining
Or for dens from which to view *The Lion King*.
His bedroom. No small warm lion cub body
Sprawled across the bed. No piles of books.
Instead she touches their narrow backs as they stand
On the shelves. Straight. Silent.
No high exuberant voice reaching for gruff villain's tones.
The kitchen. As she makes boring grown-up food
No doors swing and bang. No through draughts.
No vortex created by Hurricane Leo
Hurtling through to the garden which is empty.
No scrambling, singing shape
Swings from the lowest branch of the apple tree.

The scars of the grass from sliding tackles are starting to heal.
Only a few caveman drawings
Of motor bikes and aeroplanes
Decorate the mantelpiece
And a fat yellow ball perches
High in the clematis
Like fruit.
Like the sun.

Janet Wadsworth

GROWING UP

On the bridge of adulthood
Too uncertain of the wood
Rotten, sinking in the mud
I would miss it if I could

Turgent stream maturity
Blanket to the river's key
Cannot swim and so I flee
One day I will join the sea.

Matthew Rickard

LIFE WISH

Let me be there
To share your sunlit hours
When joy is yours and life is full.
Where beauty lies
And when your whole wide world smiles -
Let me be there.

Let me be there
To share your shadow hours
When sadness steals the daylight from your eyes.
Where sorrow falls
And while your whole world weeps -
Let me be there.

Let me be there
To share your twilight hours
When life runs short and hope is gone.
When darkness comes
And when your whole world dies -
Let me be there.

Ruth Baker

PRIMROSE

Reclining gently 'neath the aspen spray
Thy welcome presence greets my wondering eyes,
As genial Spring steals forth in light array
And from the wakening earth fresh beauties rise!

Not in some favoured, cultured garden plot
Dost thou delight to make thy loved abode;
The slighted copse thy dear selected spot
To cheer the weary traveller on the road.

Co-riser with the dawn, th' industrious bee
Draws from thy fruitful source her ample store;
Forsakes her comrades o'er the clovered lea
And leaves behind the dark and cheerless moor!

Well may the lark, from out th'ethereal blue,
Proclaim in tender tones thy matchless birth;
I haunt thy bowers 'mid late or early dew,
Thou harbinger of peace, thou star-of-earth!

Thy lovely face, in sweet endearing vein,
To me a lasting joy doth truly bring;
The friendly sunshine, and the freshening rain,
Conspire with thee to bless the opening Spring!

The am'rous sunbeams settle on thy head
As through the bursting bowers they wend their way,
Come with the morning dews that o'er thee spread,
And, lingering, fare thee well at close of day!

Thrice beauteous flower! I eulogise thy charm,
As by the gliding stream I muse on thee;
Thy chief delight the pleasing air to embalm,
And thy chief virtue-sweet humility!

William Teare

IN THE COUNTRY

Annie sat in disbelief, not that she was Lottery addicted
Merely that after years of hard work
She was in need of some relief

The numbers came up
The First
The Second
The Third
She sat quite still, not uttering a word.

The Fourth, Oh my God, could this be
More than a tenner? Let me see.
She got on the 'phone.

How much for four?
Sixty eight pounds!
And if you'd one more?
A couple of thousand her uncle did roar

Oh, I don't care Annie thought to herself
This will do fine
Sixty eight pounds is plenty
For a really good time.

A short break in the country
That's what I'll do
To visit my friends, Peter and Sue

Long walks - fresh air
And then when it ends
Back to London to try once again.

For six number this time
And the chance to win
A cottage in the country
Called *Fortune's End.*

Phyllis O'Connell

JUST SUPPOSING . . .

If a little black ant grew the size of a mouse
It would shock you to death in your shoe,
And if a tiny wee mouse grew as big as a cat
A normal sized trap wouldn't do.

If a cat, in its turn, grew the size of a fox
It would eat ten tins of tuna each day,
And if a fox stretched and stretched to become like a pig
The chickens might well get away.

If a pig grew long legs like an emu bird has
We'd have bacon that still couldn't fly,
And if that same bird got as large as a cow
Its eggs would reach up to the sky.

If a cow changed its shape to that of a shark
The milk would be all watered down,
And the shark had great horns on its head like a moose
I fear that it surely would drown.

If the moose could then possibly enlarge a bit more
To the size of a giant giraffe,
Covering it in chocolate to serve for dessert
Would seem an impossible task.

The giraffe would have to put on nineteen tonnes
To get up to an elephant's weight.
But with long neck and legs and a stomach like that
It might well have too much on its plate.

If an elephant had fins and a tale like a whale
It would never forget as it swam
That it owed its aquatic ability to
The black ant where this story began.

Sophie Tucker

CHRISTMAS MAGIC

There is a magic at Christmas time,
It's a magic that's in your heart
It makes you happy, it makes you help others,
Let's hope it doesn't depart.

You must keep it alive feed it with happiness,
Kindness love and good cheer,
And with a bit of luck that Christmas magic,
Could last throughout the New Year.

Dave 'Snappa' Snape

LOST AND FOUND

When you say your last farewells and grieve my parting - I have not gone
When you touch my cold hands and face, I return the touch with
warmth of heart.
Though my eyes are closed, they see you with a clarity of vision
unknown before.
Though your anguished whispers seems to fall on unhearing ears,
I hear the murmurs of your heart, and answer the soul within.
No, I have not gone; I am with you in all the steps you take,
I hold you close in your daily life, and talk to you in your dreams.
You have only to be quiet on waking, to know of our communion
of the night.
When you are troubled, go to a secret place and I shall find you.
Put aside your cares and wait - and I shall impart the knowing
which you seek.
For we are closer now than ever before, and I shall care for you
each day, for we two are one - now and always.

A Vince

DREADFUL WORDS

Of all the words to fill the air
And float around the room
Just one sentence short and bare
Settles like a gloom

Its icy syllables creep and twine
Like fingers round my heart
They empty out all thoughts divine
And tear my soul apart

What form of words you kindly say
Could fill your aching head
With hopeless feelings of dismay
And deep foreboding dread?

What words? Oh surely you must know
The sentence children utter
Before they even learn to grow
Or rebellion begin to mutter

They pierce the air like steely knives
And strike a note of discord
They shatter our contented lives
With: 'Mother, I'm so *bored.'*

Tanya Harris

INFORMATION

We hope you have enjoyed reading this book - and that you will continue to enjoy it in the coming years.

If you like reading and writing poetry drop us a line, or give us a call, and we'll send you a free information pack.

Write to

Arrival Press Information
1-2 Wainman Road
Woodston
Peterborough
PE2 7BU